LIFE:

CONFERENCES DELIVERED AT TOULOUSE

BY THE

REV. PÈRE LACORDAIRE,

OF THE ORDER OF FRIAR-PREACHERS.

Translated from the French, with the Author's permission,

BY

HENRY D. LANGDON,

Catholic Authors Press
www.CatholicAuthors.com

First published 1875
Reprinted 2007 Catholic Authors Press

ISBN: 978-0-9783198-5-4

Catholic Authors Press

www.CatholicAuthors.org

TO

M. A. Y.

A LOVING TRIBUTE

OF

TIME-TRIED FRIENDSHIP.

H. D. L.

DECLARATION.

ALTHOUGH I have constantly taught under the authority and in presence of the Archbishops of Paris, and my doctrine has never been criticised or called in question by them; although that same doctrine published by the press, has excited neither reproach nor discussion, yet, lest in treating so many theological questions some involuntary error may have escaped me, and this I must and do readily presume from my weakness, I declare that I submit my Conferences to the Catholic Church, whose son I am, and in particular to the Holy Roman Church, the mother and mistress of all Churches, wherein resides the plenitude of authority founded upon earth by our Lord Jesus Christ.

I also declare that I do not acknowledge the pretended reproductions of my Conferences which have been made by various periodicals, whatever be their form or name. I once more protest against the violation of literary rights whose result is to place under the name of a preacher discourses imperfectly reported amidst an immense auditory, and no less imperfectly corrected by the authors of such speculations. Should the doctrine contained in these publications be attacked, I decline the responsibility thereof as of a work which is not mine, and for which I can be held accountable only by a violation of all right and equity.

> FR. HENRI-DOMINIQUE LACORDAIRE,
> *Prov. des Fr. Prêcheurs.*

NANCY, *at the Convent of Notre-Dame-du-Chêne.
the 15th October* 1851.

CONTENTS.

	PAGE
DECLARATION	V
LIFE IN GENERAL	I
THE LIFE OF THE PASSIONS	31
THE MORAL LIFE	69
THE INFLUENCE OF THE MORAL LIFE IN LEADING MAN TO HIS END	106
THE SUPERNATURAL LIFE	143
THE INFLUENCE OF THE SUPERNATURAL LIFE UPON PERSONAL AND PUBLIC LIFE	185

LIFE IN GENERAL.

MY LORD,* GENTLEMEN,

Twenty years ago, God gave me the thought of expounding from the pulpit the body of Christian doctrine. The first part of this work is done. To-day I begin the second.

The times and places are greatly changed. Having reached this point in a laborious career, I would cast a glance upon the past and the future. Looking back upon the past, I thank God; who, in so long a course, amidst so many private and public vicissitudes, has permitted me to complete a large portion of an extensive plan. Looking towards the future, I thank him for having opened this edifice to me, where I find an auditory less numerous, doubtless, and less celebrated than before, but which has preserved the honour of religion with that of letters, the traditions of faith with those of taste and knowledge. Amongst you, Gentlemen, I shall not forget the past, but I shall not fear the future. You will be the guardians of my words, and from you, perhaps my last hearers, they

* Monsigneur Mioland, Archbishop of Toulouse.

will fall back upon those who, in other times and places, received the first fruits of my ardour. I dare not say of my apostolate.

When we treat of truth in a dogmatic point of view, the question is: What is faith, and how must we believe?

When we treat of truth in a moral point of view, the question is: What is life, and how must we live?

These two questions, although bound up together, are very different from each other.

We may despise faith, but we cannot despise life. We may refuse to submit our minds to the revealed truth of God, and against his word make an arm of the reason which we hold from him; but we cannot stand up as rebels against life, as masters of life. Whosoever you may be, you are the subjects of life. It did not wait for your orders to come to you, it will not wait for them to withdraw from you. It came to you without you; it will leave you in spite of you. It reigns by its own essence, which does not depend upon you, and which, nevertheless, you bear in yourselves as in a fragile and an immortal vessel. You live, but you live as subjects, and your power, which is so great against faith, is null against life.

I am wrong. Would to God that we had but to submit to life! By a strange contrast, however,

Life in General.

we hold this life, which is not of us, which deals with us as it pleases, in the hand of our counsel. We speak, and it listens; we command, and it obeys; and, at the same time slaves and lords, we mingle with the necessities of servitude, the responsibility of rule. We cannot be born nor can we die when we please, neither can we choose the place and conditions of our existence; but in the fatal circle where it holds us, although free in our actions, we are the willing instruments of our destiny, we answer for ourselves to our own fortune, and, whilst nature convinces us of our dependency, conscience convinces us of our sovereignty. Burdened with this double load from the day of our birth, we thus advance, masters and slaves of ourselves, to another day which is unknown to us; and beyond that day, to ages and things wherein our life appears to us from afar under that double and terrible character which it presents even here below, of necessity and liberty, of invincible duration and inevitable account. If, therefore, when I treated of faith, I spoke with certainty, I feel much more certain in speaking to you of life; my strength here derives force from your weakness, and instead of your mind being able easily to object to truth, your conscience will henceforth be my most sure helper.

What then is life? What is that mysterious power

which has been forced upon us as a stranger, and for which we must answer as for ourselves?

Often, in my youth, I have climbed high mountains. Under their solemn form they hold a charm which delights us. It seems that in raising us with them, our souls take a higher soar, a deeper scrutiny, and the poet has not said in vain;

> Jehovah has blessed the heights of earth.

We mounted then, charmed with our youth, touched by the scene which widened at each moment under our feet; but, in proportion as we mounted, light and joyous, something of nature vanished before us. The hum and flight of birds became rare, the air moved through foliage less dense; little by little even the trees fled before us in a distant perspective, and a bloomless field remained to us as a last vestige of grace and fertility. Soon nothing was left but solitude; barren, dreary, silent, without breath, and well-nigh without respiration; our own ceased also, and beholding, listening, oppressed by weariness and wonder, we exclaimed within ourselves: Nature is dead!

What then was wanting? What gave us this doleful impression? Two things were wanting: movement and fertility. Life is a fertile movement, death is sterile immobility. And as fertility always appears to us with movement, we believe that wheresoever it is, there is life. To hear or see movement, is to hear or see life; and as all moves in nature, we believe that all nature is living, even that which we call dead by comparison. For there are many degrees in movement, and therefore many degrees in life. Hardly do we dare to say, save as a poetical figure, that air and light are living, because if they move, it is under the impression of a force which, so far from being their own, does not leave to them even the shadow of individuality. They are rather the seat of life than living themselves. Under their influence, stones, minerals, metals, things obscure and inanimate, receive, nevertheless, their part of life in a subsistence which is proper to them, and wherein are hidden mysteries of affinities, increase, and relations. Above these, spreading out their roots and their branches, producing leaves, blossoms, and fruit, upon an organised stock, the plants open a more definite reign, and, in their ascensions and radiations, prepare for us a living shade, and food as pleasant as their shade. But, bound to the earth that nourishes them, they can neither obey our voice nor follow our footsteps; their captive movement holds them upon the earth whence they draw fertility. The animal seeks them there. In him life properly so called is first inaugurated, because, in him, movement, which in inferior beings was only individual, becomes spontaneous and sensible. Endowed with sight and hearing in order to know nature, with memory in order to recall his impressions, with instinct in order to desire and to shun, the animal moves upon earth if not as a king, at least as a guest, and his form is already the foreshadowing of another form which in its look and features is to express the fire of thought.

I have named man. An animal also, I see him in a flesh which moves heavily; his arms have neither the strength of the lion nor the quickness of the eagle, and in comparing them by their speed in time and space, man seems to be the subject. Nevertheless, it is he who is king. Aged and feeble at his fireside, he is still the highest life of the visible world; for he thinks, and to think is to move in the infinite. Withdraw every horizon subject to measure, every image even of earth and heaven that falls under a limit, forget number, weight, form: man thinks! With a single movement of the spirit which animates him and makes him a thinking creature, he traverses all created, all possible worlds; and alone, in the calm brightness of his reason, he conceives and names the infinite. Not the universe, but the universal appears to him; not time, but eternity; not space, but immensity. All becomes transformed under the action of his thought, and assumes an

Life in General.

extent which explains and holds all. He may be accused as a visionary; but so to accuse him would be to destroy his reason, and no living being can annihilate itself: the individual may be killed, but the race cannot; and in the race subsists the reality, which mocks at death, and truth, which mocks at negation.

Man moves in the infinite by his thought: he also moves there by his will. Whilst the animal obeys the instinct that urges him, man, stronger than his earthly appetites, commands and subjects them. By desire he dwells in the unutterable solitudes of the eternal and the immense, and his love seizes the invisible ideal of beauty. He loves as he thinks, unmeasured in his affections as in his thought, and his heart dilating like his intelligence, he feels free even under the weight of the infinite. He thinks, he loves, he is free! Such is his life, such are you all, Gentlemen; and in listening to me your conscience witnesses that I flatter neither your nature nor your destiny. Above you, doubtless, as faith teaches me, there exist spirits unclothed with flesh, purer than yourselves, having a more direct vision of truth, but not another sphere, another movement, another liberty: man, as well as the angel, has nothing above him but the infinite, real and living, that is to say, God.

Do you remember how God defined himself to Moses: EGO SUM QUI SUM—*I am who am?* Man, defining himself in his turn, has said in humbler, but almost as marvellous language: COGITO, ERGO SUM —*I think, therefore I am.* That is to say, I conceive, I name, I inhabit the infinite; therefore I have life. For whosoever does not move in that unmeasured orbit of being, possesses but a faint reflection of life, a shadow that fades and vanishes, leaving no trace behind. God defines himself by the substance of being; man by thought, which is his highest attribute, and whereby he embraces, under God, the same horizon as God.

God is the summit of life. He is its eternal and absolute act, an immutable act, immoveable even, if I may use such an expression, but of an immobility which is the first movement, because it is infinite activity subsisting in itself. For man, for all created beings, movement, which is their life, has not this quality of subsistent repose. Thought is what approaches nearest to it, for it is able, even here below, to reach the contemplation of truth. But contemplation, which is not ecstasy, does not exclude inquiry, desire, clouds, and uncertainties, and but rarely, on great occasions, does the wayfarer attain the divinity of repose in the living act of thought.

I have defined life. Life is movement, because

it is activity, and because all activity is expressed by movement more or less perfect, until it attains to immutability in God. But since life is movement, since it passes, whither does it go? Whence is it that we are not at peace within ourselves, and satisfied with being? Why does our greatest repose, even sleep, bring us only an incomplete suspension of our faculties, and that upon the couch where our limbs recline, our imagination still revolts and excites in us with dreams of action a dream of life?

It is said that in the times near to the coming of Christ, the temple of Jerusalem was filled with wondrous signs, and that a doctor of the law, on witnessing these prodigies, could not refrain from exclaiming: "O temple! O temple! What hast thou, and why art thou troubled?" And I, speaking of another temple greater than that of Jerusalem, the temple of human life, I exclaim, with the same doleful accent: O life! O life! What hast thou, and why art thou troubled? Canst thou, then, never find repose?

Evidently, all movement supposes direction, and all direction supposes an object. If we had no object, if in each of our acts and in their totality we did not suppose a term to which we tend, it would be impossible for us to move, or our movements, deprived of all meaning, would wander at hazard, foreign to all rational and mechanical direction.

Movement implies a starting-point, which is the free activity of the living being, and a point to be reached, which is something to which activity aspires, which it has not, and which it desires to have. This something is the end of life. What is it? Do you know? Children of life, heirs of time and space by your bodies, of the infinite by your souls, do you know what you desire, do you know what you do and whither you go? Ah! for myself, I know it well; for, like you, I have received at my birth the heart of a man, and the abyss which is in yours is in mine also. I know what I desire, I know what I seek; and in making my confession to you I shall make yours also. Wretched that we are, I desire, I seek, I hope, I wait for happiness. "Happiness," to use an expression of St Augustine, "is the final end of man." OMNES HOMINES CONVENIUNT IN APPETENDO ULTIMUM FINEM, QUI EST BEATITUDO.*

At this word, although sheltered by the name of St Augustine, you should stop me, and I halt of myself before a great scruple. For to say that happiness is the end of life, is to say that it is its motor, since the end determines at the same time the movement and the direction of movement. But to say that happiness is the motor of our life, is it not to confess that personal interest is the necessary

* *De Trinitate*, lib. xiii., cap. 4.

principle of all our actions? Can it then be possible that the very notion of life is the notion of egotism? Can it be possible that in defining life as *a natural and lawful movement towards happiness*, we inscribe upon the frontispiece of the moral order, and under the very guardianship of the Gospel, an appeal to that passion of self which ruins all virtue? Is man then unable to withdraw from himself, and act under the impression of another motor than his happiness, under the impression of duty? Is sacrifice refused to him save under pain of renouncing his nature and his reason; and that image of happiness, which should be only an afterthought of the mind, an ulterior consequence of justice desired and practised, shall we place it, by our definition even of life, in the first rank of our conscience, as the supreme light which, before all others, should enlighten and direct our actions?

I love in you, Gentlemen, that ready protestation of good, and I would seal it with my blood; but the logical force of ideas still withholds me, and I dare not follow you so quickly to the generous ground whereto you invite me.

Doubtless duty is a sacred notion of man, a part of his life; but is it the highest? Duty, considered in its essence, is a rule; it is the rule of our actions, but not their object. It is the way, not the term; the means, not the end. Now the means is inferior to the end; we desire the means for the end, and not the end for the means. Ask yourselves: when you perform a duty, you may forget the reward—this I grant; but is duty, how generously soever it may be performed, the last end of your life? Is it in your power to stop there, as if nothing were beyond it, either in your hope or in your thought? Does nature itself place no obstacle here to the impulsions of your heart? It does not permit you to be indifferent towards happiness, and although you are free to renounce duty, you are not free to renounce happiness. Man, whatsoever he may do, is withheld between two necessities which govern his life: the necessity of the first principles of his understanding, and the necessity of the final end of his existence. He cannot free himself from the one or the other, because the one and the other form the regular foundation of the intellectual and moral orders. Without the necessity of the first principles, man would destroy light in himself; without the necessity of the final end of his being, he would destroy his activity. He must see and hope in order to live: the son of truth and beatitude, he may go astray in the palace of his fathers, but he cannot fly therefrom.

The Gospel itself, how exalted soever it may be above nature, speaks to you on this head as nature speaks. It does not say, *Blessed are they that mourn*, without adding, *for they shall be comforted*. It does not say, *Blessed are the poor*, without adding, *for theirs is the kingdom of heaven*. Assuredly you would not aspire to higher perfection than that of the Gospel, and however great in you disinterestedness may be, it cannot be greater than in the heart of the Man-God.

And yet my soul responds to yours. I feel with you that I cannot place duty, sacrifice, the ardour of heroes and saints, on the second rank; and make the prospective of personal happiness the principle that leads me to love good. If I do not deceive myself, I love good for itself, and if happiness follow it, as it should do, I take it as a consequence, and not as the prime motor of my love. It seems to me that I should not love if I loved in order to be happy, and although happiness should be inseparable from love, I place it on the left hand, and not on the right. Such is the order which the heart teaches me, and although metaphysics with tradition assure me that happiness is *my final end*, I dare to believe that there is obscurity here which requires to be enlightened.

We will do this; we will pass this Thermopylæ of the moral order by asking ourselves: What is happiness?

But who knows happiness? Who has seen it? Who can tell where it dwells? Job said, *Whence then cometh wisdom, and where is the place of understanding? It is hid from the eyes of all living, and the fowls of the air know it not.** If this be true of wisdom, how much more true is it of happiness! Nevertheless, Job added, *Destruction and death have said, With our ears we have heard the fame thereof.* And this is true of happiness as of wisdom. We name it, we desire it, we seek it, and consequently—do not doubt it—it is not altogether a stranger to us. Yes, in this valley of our trouble, which David eloquently called a *vale of tears;* in this torrent of Cedron, which the Saviour of the world has crossed like ourselves, and from which we daily drink the bitter and troubled water of our life, happiness is not unknown to us, nor is it even absent. With man, when he fell, it passed the lost threshold of Eden, and for sixty centuries, banished like us, it wanders with us in the world, the hallowed companion of our misfortunes, the fellow-citizen of our exile. It is not permitted to appear constantly or fully before us, but it is not forbidden to choose an hour and give it to us. Sometimes it knocks at our door, sits down by our hearth, desert or filled, and with a single glance cast upon our heart, draws from it that tear whereby we learn what it is. Tear of mothers who have found their sons after absence and perils! Tear of the

* Job xxviii. 20, 21.

traveller who hails with the dawn the shores of his long-lost country! Tear of heroes between victory and death! Tear of the just man under the tremour of conscience! Tear of Augustine speaking of God to his mother by the brink of the waves which are to bear him back pure to Carthage! How many we never number, and how many more we ignore, because the heart of man, so deep for misery, is deeper far for happiness! Misery comes to him from accident, happiness from his nature and his predestination.

Now if we study the mystery that passes within us when happiness touches us for a moment, we soon find that it is caused by the satisfaction, more or less complete, of one or many of our faculties—whether of the mind, by poetry and eloquence; of the heart, by a requited affection; of the conscience, by an action that rouses it; of our whole being, by circumstances which at the same time take possession of it and draw it forth from itself. But we are so vast, our faculties are so complex and our aspirations so ardent, that in reality it never happens that the inspiration from above raises us to the point necessary to attain the fulness of ecstasy. Some part of us always remains in the shade or in disquiet, and what escapes therefrom escapes but with difficulty. Happiness comes and goes. It is the light that comes from the east and vanishes in the west. The whole earth sees it, and thrills; but it passes. It passes like youth, like beauty, like talent, like whatsoever is happy. Nevertheless, however rapid it may be, it becomes to our faculties as a satisfaction that produces repose, and to judge it by the short apparition which reveals it to us, we may define it as the repose of being in the full and inexhaustible satisfaction of all its faculties.

What conclusions shall we draw herefrom in regard to the question before us? As yet none. We know what happiness is, but not what is its source and whence it comes to us. Now, this is the main point, in order to learn whereto we aspire when we aspire to happiness, and if the movement which bears us thitherward is selfish or generous, forms for us a life which manifests itself by love or by interest.

The ancients, like ourselves, asked whence happiness comes to us. Some placed it in bodily well-being, such as the delights of the senses; others in the pleasures of the soul, such as science and glory; the more heroic, not to say the more profound, placed it in virtue. Such was the whole ladder of life among the ancients. They neither descended lower nor mounted higher. Whoever came into the world, whether he philosophised or followed instinct, chose one of these three kinds of happiness, save certain moderate men who, skilfully blending the three, proclaimed with Horace that mediocrity of desire and possession, to which remains the name of *aurea*, which the poet gave to it.

I shall say nothing of the first, of those who sought their highest good in the things and delights of the body. The poor man believes in riches, and this image seen from afar appears to him like a dream gilding his sad days, like those suns which we do not enjoy because they are lost in the rigorous serenity of winter, and which nevertheless give some idea and hope of genial warmth. But he who is able to draw near to riches and behold it in the hands of sensuality, needs no philosophy to learn the value of gold and the senses in the question of happiness; a glance is sufficient to show him human desolation in its most dramatic form. The poor sensualist has still some illusion, the rich sensualist has none. He has lost in satiety the last good of the wretched.

Shall I halt before science, glory, all the incorporal but terrestrial gifts? Alas! we have the lives of great men, it is the history of our race in its most magnificent representatives; name them, if you will, and seek in that luminous trace where they appear to us what happy days mankind might envy from their memory. Alexander died at the age of thirty; Scipio in exile; Hannibal of poison; Pompey in a snare; Cæsar at the senate, by a blow from a beloved hand; Homer is blind, and laments with Milton that he cannot see the hallowed light of which he could still sing; Tasso yields to melancholy on the eve of mounting the Capitol; Dante, his ancestor in the same glory and the same country, is so also in the same misfortune; Camoëns follows them in the distance, and from the bed of the hospital where he dies, does not even perceive the dawn of his fame. How high soever we may look in the firmament of great names, misfortune cleaves to them as a predestined satellite, and the wisdom that seeks its cause finds nothing better than that God takes pleasure in placing genius and virtue to struggle with adversity, in order, in that contrast, to witness a sight worthy of himself. These, Gentlemen, are ordinary declamations, and hardly can thought embellish them by images worthy to beguile memory.

But supposing that the pleasures of the body or the soul held in their narrow limits the secret of happiness, the doctrine that proposed them to men as the object of their life would not the less have contained two vices incapable of justification. It would, first, have overthrown the moral order by concentrating the appetites of human liberty upon things ephemeral, corrupted, moreover, by the two principal passions of our heart—namely: sensuality and pride. Nothing could correct this defect, not even the prospective of having to render an account of our actions in a higher world: for upon what could that judgment be given, were pleasure held to be the basis of the life of mankind?

Therefore, when the Gospel appeared, its first words were: *Blessed are the poor, blessed are they that weep, blessed are the clean of heart, blessed are they that suffer persecution*—not, as we have already remarked, that poverty and trouble are in themselves beatitude, but because it was necessary to bar the road where mankind ran in search of false pleasures, and show that, so far from being the end, they were not even the means thereto.

The second vice of these doctrines, always supposing the reality of happiness attached to earthly pleasures, was that it excluded nearly the whole of the human race from any possible share in happiness, that is to say, it ruined human life by placing its final end in a prospective unattainable nearly to all. For where are those among us who are rich, powerful, skilful, celebrated, endowed, in fine, with all those privileges of body and mind which the inflexible avarice of things grants to so few? Many appear in the lists, but only rare favourites rise, after the struggle, upon the obscure and mangled remains of their brethren. Therefore the Gospel, at the same time that it proclaims the narrow road of suffering, adds also: *Come to me, all of you*—VENITE AD ME, OMNES. A sublime cry come from the mouth of God made man, and which changed all regards with every horizon.

Nevertheless—I have been careful to remark it—antiquity did not halt, in the question of happiness, at the wisdom of Epicurus or Horace; it reached higher in a system which has produced its last great men, and which, chimerical as it was, is not the less worthy of our gratitude and admiration. For there are errors which honour, when the times can do no better, and when those errors are efforts of men to raise up their own times. The stoics saw clearly that neither sensible pleasures, nor the joys of the mind and self-love, could be the end of life and the seat of true happiness. They saw this by one of those chances of the heart which, after the divine word, are the great light of the world—light which produces heroes, although unable to produce saints. Appearing at the decline of Greece, when its liberty no longer existed, the stoics established virtue as the final end of man and the inviolable essence of his happiness. They willed that their sage should be free in all captivity save that of vice, and that pain itself should not draw from him the idea that it was an evil, thereby desiring to establish their sovereign independence of all the accidents of life, and to protest in the name of virtue the immutability which it gave them in the possession of real good. Rome, waxing old, and although mistress of the world no longer mistress of herself, admitted within her walls, amongst the trophies of her ancient customs, that rigorous doctrine, and with it reanimated the remains of her virility. Under emperors wearied of the baseness which they had created, there were certain souls who were not to be corrupted by fortune, and the Roman toga received from their blood, shed by tyranny, a last ray which still covers mankind, so much does a generous doctrine, even when false, bear with it the secret blessing of the God of strength and devotedness.

Stoicism had the indisputable merit, which was the cause of its greatness, of saving morals by uniting the idea of happiness to that of virtue, and at the same time rendering accessible to all the final end of man. For virtue is not, like riches, power, or glory, a privileged or an exceptional thing; it is the reign of order in every soul that wills it, the spontaneous fruit of love, which is the common fund of our nature, and the most lowly hut is an asylum as open to it as the palace of kings. A thought followed by a resolve, a resolve followed by an act: such is virtue. It is produced when we desire it, it increases as quickly as our desires, and if it costs much to him who has lost it, he has always in himself the ransom which will bring it back again. Stoicism was then a moral and a popular doctrine, and would perhaps have been considered divine if the Gospel had not been at the gates of the world, and uttered to it that great cry which the world has repeated to be forgotten nevermore.

According to stoicism, life is a movement which has liberty for principle, virtue for orbit and term. Now, there lies here an idolatry of man under a magnanimous illusion. Man, whatever he may do, is neither the principle, the orbit, nor the term of his life. He comes from beyond himself, and he seeks above himself the supreme end of his being, as a stream sprung from the depths of earth flows on to the abyss of ocean. In vain would stoicism confound virtue and happiness; in vain would its followers insult suffering and death, in order to save their doctrine; suffering and death made them great, but it did not make them happy. They suffered as heroes, they died as martyrs; sacred victims, whom philosophy crowned with flowers and the consciousness of glory, but whom reason condemned, by joining, in spite of them, the idea of impassibility and immortality to the idea of beatitude. Why should we lie to ourselves? If falsehood may become sublime, it can never become true. I do not say that pride corrupted all the virtues of the stoics: the sincere love of good may be allied to false wisdom, and false wisdom may deceive even to exaltation men of great heart. But if Thrasea, Helvidius, Epictetus, Marcus Aurelius, were sages, they were so like those trees which from corrupted earth shoot forth towards heaven venerable trunks and branches.

Where are we, Gentlemen, and what, in fine, is the home of happiness? What, beyond us and with us, is the inexhaustible seat where we shall find the living repose of all our faculties? Ah! do you not perceive it? You think in the infinite, as I said to you just now, you love in the infinite; how, out of the infinite, should you find the repose of your thought and of all your faculties? There is your principle, there also is your centre, there your term. No limited object, however beautiful, is able to appease the inner hunger that consumes you, because as soon as you possess it you have exhausted it. An invincible energy bears you beyond time and space, and happiness flies before you in the unmeasured regions which your intelligence opens to you, and whither your will necessarily follows it. But the infinite is not an abstraction without living reality; it lives, it thinks, it loves, it is free, it has a great name inscribed upon the portal of all life as the proper name of life itself;

it is called GOD. It is in GOD that happiness dwells, because in him fulness is.

It is worthy of all wonder that when the ancients, by their poets, represented the sojourn of the blessed in another world, they painted it as a calm shadow of the universe, an unsubstantial image of past things, and Virgil, animating that strange abode of happiness with his own spirit, inflicted upon it the name of *kingdom of emptiness*—INANIA REGNA. He showed there to his contemporaries happy shades regretting the light of day, and endeavouring in noiseless games to feign their by-gone combats. It is because our fathers before Christ had not the idea, so simple for us, that happiness is in God. They believed in divine justice, in the rewards and punishments of another life; they also believed, perhaps, in the disappearance of sensible matter in that other life which they imagined beyond the tomb; but that God was that life, that the soul, a living and substantial being, was in direct relations with its source, and drew therefrom, in a contemplation of eternal beauty, the reward of its beauty personally acquired by virtue, that was not of their times. The shadow of truth covered them, and they made even of known truth a gloomy and silent shadow. Mahomet coming afterwards, Mahomet initiated to the Gospel, had not even this merit. He clothed supreme happiness with flesh, and that phantom of his paradise still persecutes the shameful imagination of his followers, the only people who have not known modesty.

Happiness is in God, reason proves it, the Gospel declares it to us, and thereby falls the scandal raised within us by that definition of life: *Life is a natural and lawful movement towards happiness;* for henceforth it should be: *Life is a movement, whose principle, centre, and term is God.*

Doubtless, it remains always that happiness is our final end, since God is happiness itself; but it also remains that our last end is in perfection, since God, who is supreme beatitude, is at the same time infinite perfection. Being like him in our nature, we cannot separate in our tendencies that which is in him by the same title and in the same degree. The love of happiness is not the first cause that leads us to love good, and the love of good is not the first cause that leads us to love and seek happiness. They are two movements springing within us from a single source, contemporary in their expansion, equal in their power, and which, aiding one another upon earth, have both, after a time of trial, their immutable satisfaction in God. During that trial, withdrawn from good by corruption or weakness, we may be brought back to it by the fear of losing our final beatitude; but that fear, however great it may be, is not in our heart the root of justice and goodness, and if we halt there without raising up from the depth of our being the true and disinterested love of order, we shall not save ourselves from condemnation. *Fear is the beginning of wisdom,* says the Scripture; it is not wisdom itself, it does not give back to the soul its purity and beauty, its taste for uprightness, its delight in the intimate likeness to God, its legitimate aspiration, in fine, towards the total destiny of man, which is perfection as well as happiness, or rather happiness by perfection.

Even during the trial, there is a difference between these two essential and co-ordinate elements of our life which it behoves us so much the more to remark, as they will complete the explanation of the fundamental difficulty which we purposed to solve. The love of happiness is not free in us, it is inevitable; on the contrary, the love of good, so natural as it is to our heart, leaves to it the fulness of its liberty; it is obligatory without being compulsory: and we can conceive that it should be so, since without liberty, good, not being our work by any title, would remain impersonal to us. It is the free choice between good and evil that restores to us the proper use of our faculties, and raises us, although having received all, to the dignity of responsible and sovereign beings. We are just because we will to be so, and that will being applied to our actions, our whole life escapes from fatality, save by these two extreme points, the first principles of our understanding and the invincible desire for happiness. But that love of good is moderated by the moral obligation of performing it, and thence it comes that the love of truth, justice, virtue, which is innate to us, appears to us under the form of duty. Duty is not its essence, it is but its passing form, and therefore that divine love is not only our rule, it is also our nature and our end, it is so as much as happiness, and, like happiness, it has in God its principle, its centre, and its repose.

It is therefore incorrect to say: Duty is the rule of our life, it is not its end. This is true of duty, as duty; but this is not true of good, as good; it is not true of the justice and goodness which God, in creating us, has placed in the depths of our being, and which should some day be satisfied in the justice and goodness whence they spring, according to that prophecy of the Gospel: *Blessed are they that hunger and thirst after justice, for they shall have their fill!* The Gospel, in those famous beatitudes, the foundation of Christian morals and life, not only says to us, *Blessed are you for yours is the kingdom of heaven;* it says at the same time, *Blessed are you, for you shall have your fill of justice.* Justice is then the end as well as happiness, or rather, they embrace each other in the perfect and substantial unity of God, an ocean whence we come and whither we shall return, whence we come with the love of good and the love of happiness, whither we shall return by the weight of the one as by the weight of the other, without the desired happiness destroying in us the innate disinterestedness of good, without the innate disinterestedness of good taking from us the hope of the happiness desired.

Such is life. Stoicism saw but the half of it. It saw, and this will be its glory in all ages, that virtue, which is the love of good ruling all things in our soul, is a necessary part of man, his highest and most sacred part; but it did not see, because God was hidden from it or rather because it hid God from itself, that virtue alone, in its purely human orbit, is not our true and last end. It desired to make of man a God by the efficacy of virtue, instead of making of God by virtue the good of man. Thanks to the Gospel, all the veils are drawn aside, we see life as it is, and our heart, which is its vase, is filled at the same time with the sacrifice that makes the saints, and the hope that consoles them; with the humility that annihilates them, and the glory that raises them even to God.

# THE LIFE OF THE PASSIONS.

MY LORD, GENTLEMEN,

We have sought and found the true notion of life. Life being activity expressed by movement more or less perfect, and all movement, of what kind soever, having a direction determined by an end, we cannot take account of human life without knowing the term to which it tends. Now, enlightened at the same time by the light of reason and the Gospel, we have seen that the final end of our existence is happiness, but invisible happiness which is in God alone. Thereby we have shut out from legitimate life, that is to say, from moral life, every principle of egotism; for to aspire to God as an end, is to aspire to something universal which is the inalienable good of every human creature who wills it; it is to aspire to perfection, which includes all justice and all goodness as well as all beatitude, and towards which we cannot tend without the movement which bears us thitherward possessing a generous character.

But if God be the end of our life, as it is proved, we should not only tend towards him, we should tend towards him and unite ourselves to him; for, without such union, man would be but the eternal toy of a deceptive desire; he would advance towards the infinite by a false road, like a traveller who afar off sees the desert covered with shade and freshness, but who vainly follows upon sand the imaginary track of his resting place. Man and God should somewhere and at some time meet together; they should know each other, and God should open to man the heart wherein he was conceived in love. This union, necessary to the fulfilling of our destiny, entails the consequence that man should take in God something of the divine nature; for two beings which have nothing in common could not unite together, and they could have nothing in common without possessing something of the same nature. Even then as God became man by the assumption of humanity, man, in order to enter into the possession of God, which is his final end, should on his side be invested in some way with divinity. I say in some way, in order to soften an expression which, all exact though it be, carries with it an appearance of usurping boldness. But I am encouraged by recalling those forcible expressions of the apostle St Peter: *God hath given us most great and precious promises, that by these you may be made partakers of the divine nature.** Observe that he does not say *partakers of*

---

* 2 Pet. i. 4.

divine happiness; nor does he say *partakers of eternal life.* These words are found in every page of the Gospel; he says much more, and in a sense which excludes nothing, *partakers of the divine nature,* that is to say of its perfection, and consequently of its justice and goodness. This expressly confirms the doctrine established in our preceding Conference, that the final end of man is not happiness only, but perfection.

We must attain to performing in God, under a spiritual form, the two acts which our body performs here below in the sensible atmosphere; transported to the divine atmosphere, God must become our lifegiving breath, we must receive him as the light and heat of our transfigured being, and breathe from him a breath which is his own and ours, his life and our life, his peace and our peace, his eternity and our eternity. Whilst Pagan antiquity, although it made gods of all things, dared only to give to two men the solemn name of divine, and said the *divine Homer* and the *divine Plato,* all of us, without exception, are called to that title. And to the first child whom I meet in the street, I may truly say, "My child, art thou not a human being?—Yes. Then thou must be a divine being, since such is thy right and thy destination." Nevertheless, should this name still alarm you, and seem like a distant echo of Paganism, I will say to you in the very language of Scripture something perhaps yet more astounding.

The vision of the inner heavens has twice been opened to the prophets: once in the Old Testament, to the eye of Isaias; a second time, in the New, to the eye of St John, and behold what the one and the other saw and heard: There was a throne, and upon the throne one sitting, and voices cried to one another, *Holy, Holy, Holy, Lord God Almighty.** This before God was the whole voice of heaven and earth, all the voice of spirits and worlds, all the sound, in fine, of the creature speaking to the Eternal. SANCTUS, SANCTUS, SANCTUS!—*Holy, Holy, Holy!* The sole title given by the chorus of souls to their Father as perfect praise, and the expression which exhausts glory in created tongues. This same title is ours, and St Paul, writing to the first Christians, said to them, "To you, Romans; to you, Corinthians; to you, Galatians; to you, Ephesians; to you who are called to be holy, or saints, VOCATIS SANCTIS." We may, indeed, forfeit this name which is attributed to us as to God, but we cannot deprive ourselves of it as our right or heritage, and, when we shall one day sing it, should such be our merit, we shall be saints, or holy, who will praise the Holy One in the common glory of one and the same perfection and happiness.

* Isa. iv. 3; Apoc. iv. 8.

But you readily understand that we cannot reach so far without meeting with obstacles. No road is free from them, this less than the rest, since it leads higher than all the others. There are then before us in the road of life, difficulties to overcome. What are they? These I purpose to show you to-day.

Hardly does man know himself, or even before he knows himself, when he feels the indefinite aspiration for happiness awakening within him, and at the same time there opens before his eyes the large and double field where he seeks its satisfaction. He sees the world in the field of space, and, beyond the visible world, one still more spacious, which contains the first, and of which the first is but the shadow and the radiant portico. These two worlds are sacred: one is God, the other is his work and his image. Both belong to man: nature is his, and he can also say of God: My God! Thus placed from the dawn of his reason, with one foot upon the created ground, another upon the uncreated, offspring of the one by his body, and of the other by his soul, man sees and recognises them only as possessing rights over them; he feels possessed of ability to attain them, power to secure possession of them, and draw from them his beatitude. For in vain would he see and aspire to them as the seat of his life, if he were not endowed with strength sufficient to appropriate them to himself.

So it is. Strengthened outwardly with two arms which may bear the sword and the sceptre, he has within him a double faculty at the service of his aspirations. One, the first and the noblest, has a great name: it is called Liberty. It is the gift of willing without any other cause than himself, the gift of choosing his thought, his love, his action, his destiny in fine, and of commanding himself above all others. A sovereign power, liberty lies in our inmost depths, in an abode as calm as truth; thence it beholds the two worlds that speak to us, confronts them, judges them, is silent for a moment, and then chooses between earth and God.

If liberty were alone, man would perhaps never deceive himself in his choice. He would tend to God as to his natural term by a free but unerring movement, and the visible world would be to him but a passage and a trial, as indeed it should be. But, in the decrees of creating Providence, another power was to stand at the portal of our liberty, a sentry which was not an enemy, but which has become one, and which rather attacks than guards the holy of holies of our soul: this is passion. For it was doubtless impossible, that in presence of two worlds open before us, in presence of divine and created beauty, man should remain cold, like a spirit without flesh and heart; it was indeed needful that he should love in order to be like

The Life of the Passions.

God, and love having once entered into his heart, all passion abode there with it. Passion is the faculty of being moved, and there is nothing that has not power to move us, because there is nothing that does not contain, at least in appearance, some of that happiness which is the end of our life. Shadow, light, an autumn leaf borne along by the wind, a look, a smile, all act upon us, all at least may act upon us, and raise up tempests within us which the ocean itself knows not.

Liberty, passion: liberty, a calm and commanding power; passion, a weakness, timid and subject; behold the two faculties placed in our hands by God that we may conquer heaven and earth, apparent and real beatitude.

You thought, perhaps, that liberty alone was our arm, and passion our obstacle; it is not so. The one and the other were pure in the beginning, both were given to us as sisters—liberty to choose, passion to love. But the second has seduced the first, and daily it still produces in us that work which turns us aside from our road, and which I must now expose to you.

When, either by liberty or passion, we enter into possession of God or nature, a phenomenon is produced within us which we call joy, and which is, as it were, the dawn of happiness. Joy is a dilation and an exaltation of the soul. For God—who is the end of our life—being greater and higher than we are, our soul was formed to dilate and delight in possession of Him, and this movement is wrought in our soul even when it errs, and when instead of uniting to God, its true end and beatitude, it cleaves to some object which cannot satisfy, because it cannot fill it. A false joy is the result of that error, a joy which soon vanishes, and leaves to the soul, intoxicated for a moment, only the feeling of a greater void. Nevertheless there was joy, because there was a dilation and an exaltation of our being.

There may be even more than joy, for it is of the nature of happiness to be eternal, to have neither day, nor night, nor past, nor present, nor future; and the soul predestined to that immutability of rapture has received the marvellous germ of it in its creation. On certain occasions it may feel one of its rays, and receive from its deceptive and fleeting delight as it were an illusion of eternity; this is ecstasy. Ecstasy has its name in every language, and consequently it is a reality, for nothing is named by man but what is known to him. What then is ecstasy? Ecstasy is joy in which we forget time and ourselves. Doubtless you have sometimes said: "Time passed away!" This seems very simple, and yet it is marvellous, for it means to say: "I lost all account of time; I lived, and did not feel it; I lived, and the succession of past, present, and future, ceased for my soul; for a quarter of an hour I had an apparition of eternity." Yet more; you have perhaps said: "I forgot myself!" What an expression for an egotistical being! And yet, it is true, man forgets himself; he forgets himself when he is happy; he forgets himself at the moment of the greatest dilation of his existence. It is because God, who is his true happiness, has in fact created him to forget himself one day in Him; to lose there, not his proper life and personality, but every other sentiment than that of the divine beauty and presence. Now, even here below, not only for the saints, who enjoy a foretaste of invisible beatitude in a premature possession of God, but for those of us who are sinners or moderately good, there are ecstasies because there are thrilling joys. A mother forgets herself on the return of her son; she gazes at him, touches him, clasps him in her arms; it is indeed her son, and the hours glide on for her in the charm of that stream which bore memory away.

Therefore, all of us, taught by experience or by instinct, seek for ecstasy, as the highest ideal of happiness. The saints find it in God, who is, in fact, its source; withdrawn from the world in prayer and contemplation, they also forget time, the world, themselves, and feel sometimes raised far above the narrow sphere which they inhabit with us. But, alas!

it is not so high that fallen man naturally seeks this precious good which was familiar to him in the innocence of the terrestrial paradise. As soon as he left it, his soul still full of the raptures of its youth, his lips still sweet with the remembrance of the tree of life, he asked the ruins of nature if no traces are left to them of their first efficacy. He found them there. The passions strengthened, multiplied in becoming refined; and civilisation, which is the progress of all things, brought deeper knowledge of ecstasy with a wider discovery of the secrets of life.

It is not my intention to describe to you all the modes of enjoyment in forgetfulness of ourselves. They are almost immeasurable, at least if we consider them in their degrees. But putting aside the greater part, such as ambition and avarice: ambition, which seeks ecstasy in the government of men, and is the passion of great souls; avarice, which seeks it in the possession of gold, and is the passion of the most shallow hearts; I shall speak principally of the ordinary things, of those vulgar passions which snatch the multitude from God, and from age to age hand them over to the ready emotions of flesh and blood. This is a sad portal of human life. But we cannot avoid it. Like those savage watch-dogs that guard the entrance to inhospitable dwellings, so are the passions at the gates of man, and before entering the luminous regions of his being we must pass by the barkings of his vices.

The first gift of God to the body of Adam, after He had formed him with His hands, was this: *Behold, said He, I have given you every herb bearing seed upon the earth, and all the trees that have in themselves seed of their own kind, to be your meat.** A marvellous gift, which made of all nature the table of man, and drew his blood from the veins of the universe, establishing, by that transformation of substance, a sublime relationship between him and all beings. But amongst those seeds and fruits so diverse in form, smell, and taste, there were two destined to become one day for us the active symbols of eternal life, and which contained in their privileged preparation, a more striking power under a more perfect taste; they were bread and wine, the ancient offering which the first pontiff presented in homage to the first patriarch of the old law. Bread, a generous but peaceful substance; wine, still more generous, and which, according to the very expression of Scripture, had received from the Creator the mission of *making glad the heart of man.*† Man, in fact, when he lifted the beneficent cup to his lips, found a mysterious affinity between the draught and his soul, and that melancholy—that sad veil which has covered us within

* Genesis i. 29. † Psalm ciii. 15.

since sin came, fell little by little before the repairing influence of the potent draught. It was like a revelation of that invisible food upon which the saints live in heaven, and which in the youth of God, gladdens the immortality of their own. But the more precious the gifts, the more is virtue necessary rightly to use them. We made a wrong use of this gift. Pushing to the extreme point our experience of its strength, we not only found our heart enlarging and its clouds disappearing, but reason, that importunate guest which alarms us with truth; conscience, that other witness which raises up within us the painful image of ourselves; both vanished under the unforeseen charm of the poison: we felt the ecstacy of intoxication.

It is not alone the savage on the shores of the icy lakes of the pole, who eagerly receives, in exchange for his natural treasures, the substance which he calls *fire-water*. Civilised man himself does not disdain to sacrifice his intelligence to the degrading forgetfulness of his misfortunes. We see the poor, the poor of great nations, hurrying no longer after *bread and shows*, as in the time of the Roman Empire, but to the ignoble door where lucre sells to him, at the price of his toil, a moment of shameful fascination. So much does man need to forget himself, so much does reason weigh upon him, when God does not bear in his heart its heavy load. Therefore it is not the poor only who dishonour civilised nations by seeking emotion and peace in the voluntary degradation of drunkenness; the rich, surrounded by the splendours of art, yield to these abject tastes, and the devouring remorse of its emptiness urges them like the people, to the same compensations of life. What do I say? The liberal cultivation of thought by science and letters is not always a shelter which saves the heart from so deep a degradation. Light, when it is not according to God, has its own avenging bitterness, and the mind so suffers as to delight in escaping therefrom to the ecstatic loss of reason.

Beyond all created substance, in the ideal region of the abstract, lies a power cold, impassible, inexorable, which is in regard to the things of the material order what the Destiny of antiquity was for the moral order; it is the mathematical law, the law of number, extent, force, which governs the arrangement of the inanimate world, and sustains with its immutable sanction that which has neither sentiment, will, liberty, nor life. Who would have said that even there, at the cold hearth of calculation, man would find another element of joy and ecstacy to quench his thirst for happiness? Yet he has done so. Amongst those certain rules of number and movement he has discovered combinations which engender chances without engendering certainties, and chance has appeared to him as the sovereign god of a phase of happiness, for chance responded to one of his greatest wants, the dramatic want of his nature. That same man, who loves repose and seeks it in intoxication, wills also, because he is living and free, to create an action for himself, an action which rouses him by a great interest, holds him in suspense by a tie independent of his will, and, in fine, elevates or crushes him by a sudden turn of fortune. Every other drama is foreign to him. If he witness the scenes of Sophocles or Corneille, it is not himself who is the victim or the hero; he weeps over distant misfortunes which art has raised up in order to move him; but here it is himself, when he wills, as he wills, in the measure that pleases him. Chance and cupidity blended together make for him of gambling a drama personal, terrible, and joyous, wherein hope, fear, joy, and sadness succeed one another, or rather become confounded almost at the same moment, and hold him panting under a fever which rises even to madness; for, if we say the passion of wine, we say the frenzy of gambling.

A popular frenzy like the other! But whilst the progress of taste amongst civilised nations leads in certain classes to that sobriety which forms a part of honour; gambling, stronger than civilisation, outlives the reforming movement of ages, and seems, especially in the rich, to be an inalienable appanage of mankind. It passes from the region of pleasure to that of business; political events bring to it favourable or adverse chances; and victory or defeat, in deciding the fate of empires upon battle fields, decide also the rise of a family or its fall.

Is this all? Has nature spoken its last word to us in this banquet of the passions so skilfully prepared for us? Is it satisfied with its power over us, and, in the abyss of its secrets, is there not a temptation to happiness still reserved for us?

Here, Gentlemen, I am alarmed at what I have to say, and my thought, withheld as it is in my bosom, fears itself and trembles to appear. I shall utter it nevertheless. I shall speak it under the eye of God, sure that it is my duty, and that yours also, which is to listen with modesty and respect, will not fail to help me.

It is not beyond man, between earth and heaven, it is not in the substances capable of troubling reason, or in the tragedies of chance, that we find the strongest seduction of man, his highest joy and his most poignant ecstasy. Not beyond and around him, but within himself, within the living circle of his personality, he encounters a palpable flesh, an animated and sensible flesh, which holds to his soul, which receives its orders, but which in its turn acts upon it and offers to it a field to which it may call life from the very bosom of God. For God has not given us life for ourselves alone, as a miserly treasure, incapable of giving itself. Life is, of its nature, fertile; it comes from an inexhaustible source, and in its own course spreads out in endless generations. He then who gave it to us, the God who said to all that is: *Increase and multiply*, gave still more to his highest creature the command to live beyond himself by transmitting himself to a posterity. But this command, divine for all, was higher still for us. For in others it was given only to a body, to an organisation composed of parts which could separate and find in their division a seed of themselves. Here, in man, the seat of life was the soul. The soul, one, single, indivisible, incapable of separating in order to give itself, possessing in fine, like its author, the necessity of being whole or of not being. At that supreme degree of existence he needed then a paternity like that of God, and as God in the inaccessible light of his essence, said to himself speaking to another than himself: *Thou art my son, to-day have I begotten thee*, it was needful that man, first soul, and secondly body, should, at the same time and in the same act, evoke a soul and a body living in his own likeness, and be able also to say to them like God: Thou art my son, to-day have I begotten thee. An heroic moment which man has corrupted with all the rest, and in which, under the chaste veils of affection, he has found the secret of an intoxication without honour, without power, without life, but which goes far beyond frenzy; for if we say the frenzy of gambling, we say the delirium of voluptuousness.

What had not God done in order to raise this mystery to the height of its nature and its end! The sacred union of souls under the immortal yoke of a love freely promised, pleasures and duties for ever in common, misfortunes borne together, joys of paternity tempered by concern for the future, an unspeakable mixture of blessings and troubles, virtue everywhere to sustain the weaknesses of the heart against the caprices and chances of years; but man is more skilful in his corruption than Providence in his prudency. He has burst his bonds, rejected his obligations, and from the very sources of life he draws forth death with sensuality, the great and immeasured cup of the most facile and popular of all the passions! For, in the others, man does not suffice to himself; he needs gold to procure the ecstasy of intoxication; he needs it also to excite and forget himself in the drama of gambling; and the satisfactions of pride require it still more. But here man needs only himself; he is at the same time the theatre, the object, and the instrument of his passion, and as the last word of truth in the prophecy of St John is: *And he that thirsteth, let him come, and he that will, let him take the water of life freely,** the last word of fallen nature in opening to mankind the abyss of depravity is: Come, and drink freely. Ah! thought fails me, and I am as it were seized with giddiness at this height to which vice has led me, and whence, in its bygone history and present reign, I contemplate the shipwreck of souls. Like you, the son of liberty and passion, with one foot upon that abyss which has been mine and which may soon be so again if the grace of God should desert me, I feel dizzy and trembling, my vision is troubled, and my hand seeks the stone with which Saint Jerome struck his breast, when that great man, in the depths of the desert, unsecured by labour and solitude against the remembrances of his youth, thought he saw the beauties of pagan Rome pass to and fro before his gray hairs again to invite and dishonour them.

But has not man at least found in this road the happiness he sought? Steeped in passions, is he content with himself, and does the God who looks down up him from a cross present to him a spectacle of misery unknown to him, or is it the faithful representation of his misfortunes that God has taken upon

* Apoc. xxii. 17.

The Life of the Passions.

Himself in order to instruct and reclaim him? It is important that we should know: for although the final end of man is not happiness only, but perfection and happiness, if the passions rendered him really happy here below, it would be an arm against the doctrine of life, such as the Gospel teaches us, whose importance I shall not disguise from you.

Let us then examine the world, and weigh its happiness; for ages it has laboured for happiness. Nature, in the course of time, has not been able to hide from the world any of her secrets; it has penetrated them all, applied all to its profit, and as to the passions, it is manifest that, notwithstanding the difference of times and morals, none have ever failed towards it. The world is at the age of manhood; you may promise it more prosperous times than those which it has enjoyed, but not another soul, another body, another earth, another heaven, and consequently the condition which all these elements of its life have made for it in the hands of its passions cannot essentially differ from the condition which they will make for it in the future. I listen then to the sound of the world. As a shepherd wandering in a deep and silent forest sometimes hears a sigh produced by the effort of the rising wind, so the world has voices that rise from its generations, and each of us, lost in the crowd, may in his own thoughts hear the sound of his fathers and his contemporaries. What is it? Is it a lamentation? Is it a hymn? Tell me yourselves, you, a part of the world, tell me what sound life renders to you in the secret of your conscience. But perhaps you are its happy ones, and, however vast this assembly may be, perhaps, on account of rank and wealth, it does not know the misfortunes of mankind because it does not feel their weight. Let us leave this place, not to see man, but to see him in all the reality of his destiny. Behold him; ah! yes, behold him! It is indeed he whom the Roman proconsul eighteen hundred years showed to the people, his shoulders covered with blood and purple, his hands bound to a sceptre of reed, his head surrounded with thorns woven as a crown. I know him again. Ages have not changed thee, my son; thou bearest the same mantle, the same sceptre, the same crown, and if the cross no longer waits for thee, it is because thou hast never ceased to be nailed to it.

Need I say more to you on this subject? What are images before realities? The greatest lovers of man and of his passions do not accuse us of overdrawing the picture of his miseries; they reproach us only with not prophesying their end. They say that the earthly paradise is not behind man but before him, and that he has but to advance in order to reach it and find there his repose. All the systems of philosophy, and all parties, are agreed as to human suffering, they are hostile only as to its cause and its remedy. Now especially, from a feeling of brotherhood which has sprung from Christianity, attention is more fully awaked than ever to the magnitude of our ills. The prosperous under Paganism troubled themselves but little about them: withdrawn as far as possible from the holocaust which consumed mankind, their view reached only themselves, and the groanings of the rest came to them only as the instrument or the seasoning of their pleasures. The Christian ages have brought other sentiments. Those who enjoy think of those who suffer, and the tears of the poor, gathered in the hands of charity, fall upon the hearts of the rich to purify them. We believe in adversity, and we would destroy it as far as Providence will permit us. But, in order to destroy, or at least to lessen it, we must know its cause. The Gospel accuses the passions; others accuse the vices of social organisation; it is one of the great contests of this age.

Assuredly, the ordinance of society is not a stranger to the blessings and misfortunes of human life. Even as a body derives from its organs, if they are rightly disposed, an element of well-being and duration, the body of the human race finds in just laws a means of strength, greatness, and prosperity. But are there laws that resist morals, and morals that resist passions? Laws are the expression of the reigning will, morals the result of the hearts of all, and if the hearts of all are corrupt, what must be the state of morals? The morals of pride are ambition, hatred, revenge, scorn of the poor, homicide, and war; the morals of voluptuousness are the degradation of the senses and the intelligence, the dishonour of youth, the oppression of woman, the dissolution of the marriage-bond and of family. What is to be done with a people fallen into such morals, and what organisation would spread peace and happiness amongst them? Therefore the object of all legislation, up to the present day, has been not so much to regulate interests as to govern passions; not only to establish a material order, but to found honour and virtue. This was the work of Solon, as well as of Moses, and the law of the Twelve Tables spake from the capitol like the holy ark on Sinai. The only difference was in their measure and elevation. Human law may have failed from ignorance and weakness, but everywhere, in proclaiming rights, it has proclaimed duties.

Now, what is the proclamation of duties—that proclamation without which no human society has lived for a single day—but the declaration that man has sacrifices to make? And why has man to make sacrifices, if it be not because his passions are opposed to the general good? For, if they were not so opposed, in what interest, and by what right, could he be called upon to sacrifice them? He should sacrifice them, because it results from common experience that they are contrary to the general well-being. Doubtless the human law is far less rigorous than the divine law; it could not, even if it would, be otherwise. The heart is a sanctuary which it knows not, and, powerless to command it, it shuts its eyes to the mysteries enacted there as towards actions which do not too directly attack the order of which it is the sanction. But its voice does not the less accord with the voice of God in accusing the passions of the evils of the human race. The world is not happy—all men agree in declaring it—and, by the organ of the laws that govern them, all confess also that the passions through which they seek their happiness are the source of the miseries under which mankind struggles.

It is true that, in these later times, a school, if so it may be called, has not feared to throw back upon the laws themselves the evils produced by the passions. It has said of the inclinations of nature, without excepting any, that they are lawful, and even sacred, in the eyes of truth, and that evil arises only from a default of regularity and harmony in their satisfaction. Suppose a crime to issue from pride or sensuality, it is a crime only by the law which is an obstacle to it, and has not found its place and its utility in the organisation of wants. Shall I notice such metaphysics of depravity? One of the elements of human thought and life—the notion of duty—is here denied: now every doctrine that denies an element of man, whatsoever it may be, is not a doctrine, but a conceit, which would be simply ridiculous if it could not become dangerous.

Mankind lives under laws, laws are based upon the idea of duty, duty supposes sacrifice, sacrifice applies to the most cherished inclinations of man, leaving to him intact his reason only, whereby he himself acknowledges and blesses the sword which wounds his being in order to save it.

Such is the judgment of the human race upon the passions; it adores them in its heart because its heart is corrupt; it seeks its happiness in them, because it fears to go to God, who is its invisible seat, but combats them in its codes, because in fine it must live, and, all blind though it be, it is not blind enough to misunderstand, in the common calamities, the ravages of its corruption. It is not then the Gospel only that speaks here to you, but yourselves, your laws, your customs, public opinion, reason manifested in the

The Life of the Passions.

greatest and most enduring works, all, in fine, save that which does not perish even in you, the evil which you received with life, and which you will transmit with life to your posterity.

But was it needful, in order to convict the passions of being the authors of our evils, to appeal circuitously to the testimony of legislations which have repressed their excesses? Can we not seize upon them in action, either in history, surrounding us, or within ourselves? Are not their terrible stigmas everywhere visible, and are arguments needed where the vision is seized with such living realities? Not only do you see your evils, you see also their cause: it has been one of the designs of God that the cause should reveal itself under the phenomenon which it produces. Behold, then!

Who is that young man? Whence is it that his look is dull, his cheeks are pale and hollow, his lips sad, his head heavy? Youth is the spring-time of beauty; God, who is ever-young because he is ever-beautiful, has willed that in our early years we should show something of the physiognomy of His eternity. The brow of the young man is the resplendence of the brow of God, and it is impossible to behold a virginal soul upon a pure visage without being moved with sympathy full of tenderness and respect. Now God has taken this great gift—this gift which precedes merit, but not innocence—from those who abuse it in the precocious passions which I will not any longer even name. Vice stamps its image upon that brilliant flesh which touched the heart; it traces upon it shameful lines, premature and accusing wrinkles, an air of decrepitude which is neither a mark of time, nor of the meditations of a man given to austere duties, but the certain sign of depravity which has passed by, destroying. The furrow deepens with the shame, and we see those shadows appear among us, transparent and empty, as if the last judgment had already overtaken them, and presented them unveiled to the scorn of earth and heaven.

So is it with all our passions; each has its earthly and revealing punishment, destined to teach us that their road is false, and that happiness is not at the term of the joys which they bring to us. If voluptuousness destroys youth and life, gambling wrecks the most secure fortunes amidst grievous agonies, and intoxication, by constantly attacking reason, debases the intelligence whose first light it is, and lowers it to a state of stupidity which animality would disdain. Pride, which seems more cold, has however storms hidden under its icy surface, like those polar seas where the winds have perhaps less power and action, but which, at certain moments, dissolve their inert masses, and seem to announce to the world the

The Life of the Passions. 59

sinking of its foundations. Hatred and revenge brood under discontented pride, and deceived ambition has painful shocks which wound fallen men even to death. These, Gentlemen, are our daily spectacles within ourselves and without. Our soul is its first theatre, the world shows it to us enlarged, and history, faithful to the orders of God, writes upon the ruins of Tyre and Babylon the desolations of the past and threats against the future.

But the ordinary evils of man and mankind were not sufficient to teach us the end of the passions. God has prepared other warnings for them. In all things there is a catastrophe. Even as life ends in death; as a drama closes by a climax which is the result of the complications invented by the mind of the poet; so, in the drama of the passions turned aside from God, there must be a supreme shock, something striking, terrible, before which every curse must fade, even the sign of Cain, the first murderer, in order that every reasonable creature should be unable to doubt that life and happiness are not there, but that there, on the contrary, is the road of ruins which are never restored. Young men who hear me this morning, and who this evening will listen to your vices, you will not all be struck by the thunderbolt. The ancients said that it affects to fall on the high tops, as if the masters of the thunder were jealous of their height, or would, in striking them, give a lesson to pride; so is it with whatever is extraordinary. There is in misfortune, as in genius and virtue, a sublime point which all men do not reach, and it is rare to be the chosen victim of a great expiation. I know not then which among you must pay the ransom of others to the justice of God; but when the night of Egypt comes, when the destroying angel passes, he will know more than I know, and he will not be deceived about those who are already predestinated for him. Before that night, however, before that sword which advances unseen by any, you may still hear me and reflect upon yourselves.

You have felt it, the joy which springs from the passions is not final. As soon as the intoxication is over, painful amazement, a void bitterly felt, remains in the soul. It may be filled again by new emotions; but it happens that it is reproduced more vast than before, and that painful succession between extreme enjoyment and deep dejection, between gleams of happiness and powerlessness to be happy, at length produces a constant state of sadness. The mystery of sadness is the opposite to that of joy. Joy results from a dilation and an exaltation of the soul; sadness contracts the heart and lessens it. Say not to the man who is attacked by it: Behold this beautiful day! Say not: Hear this sweet music! Say not even to him: I love you! Light, harmony, love, all that is charming and good, does but irritate his hidden wound. He is devoted to the shades, and all appears to him as in a sepulchre where there is no air, and whose marble stifles him.

But this is only the dawn of expiation. As joy is not the term of happiness felt, sadness is not the term of unhappiness tasted. Beyond joy is ecstasy; beyond sadness is despair. A moment comes when all the powers of man, satiated, give him the invincible certainty of the world's nothingness. This universe so vast, the shadow of the infinite, in falling into a heart which has no more space—loses its own. Formerly the forlorn being needed but half a smile to open before him unbounded visions; now the adoration of earth would not touch him. He would judge it as it is—as nothing. For it is not conception that is wanting to him; he is in the full brightness of his understanding. It is not even truth, for the truth of the universe is nothing. What is wanting to him, is to believe and to be moved—is to see God behind things, and to feel, under the vestment which hides Him from us, the unction of His beauty. He does not feel it. Unlike that living man who was bound to a corpse, it is he who is dead. He transports his misery to the life which oppresses him, and the palpitations of reality are no more for him than the tickings of a clock which measures his agony. It may be thought, so terrible is this voluntary suffering, that it does not exist; but, alas! despair, like ecstasy, is named in every tongue, and daily in a celebrated action, which is at the same time its proof and its effect, we have but too authentic a witness of it, if it be true that blood shed is the last seal of truth.

Despair has its martyrdom. When man no longer believes in the present world, and when the future has not appeared to sustain him, life becomes an insupportable burden. What is it to live when all is dead? What is it to live when truth no longer touches the mind, nor love the heart; when the senses themselves disdain voluptuousness, that last asylum of hope and faith? A look fixed, but without vision, holds the despairing one in a state of immobility. He listens, and no sound reaches him; no friend opens his door, no hand any longer touches his own. An infinite sense of being forsaken answers to the forlorn condition which he has brought upon himself. It is then that the angel of judgment lifts his sword; but he will not strike—his orders are not to strike. The guilty one must be the executioner, and endure, in suffering without remorse, a life without value.

You may perhaps think that this is the catastrophe which I announced as the supreme punishment of the passions. It is not so. There is a remains of human greatness in despair, because there enters into it contempt for all created things, and consequently a sign of the incomparable extent of our being. Even suicide, cowardly as it is, by the abdication of the duty of living, which includes all the others, is nevertheless an act of liberty and of high sovereignty over ourselves. Examples of this have been witnessed which have not seduced posterity, but which have drawn from it, as it were, a desire for pardon. God and man need another vengeance, a vengeance wherein the shame will be without measure, and the example without parallel. Death, whatever it may be, is but the separation of the soul and the body, the painful vestibule of immortality. There is another death, a living death, which reaches not only the bond of the two substances which form our personal unity, but which, falling upon the spirit alone, finds again there the possibility of a ruin, and knows how to produce it. O power of evil and of nothingness! Unspeakable misfortune of this great work which God has made in man! We have seen kings fall, glory fade away, Homer led by a child, Belisarius holding out his helmet for alms; but the divine ray remained still upon the brows of the blind poet and the uncrowned kings. Men might pity, but they still admired them: it was the sun sunk upon the horizon, but leaving behind the twilight of evening, the promise of morning dawn. Even in the fallen angel, as tradition tells us, there remains something of his lost majesty, and that under the scars of the thunderbolt, the eye discerns the past greatness of the first-born of spirits. Why has God prepared for us a fall in which nothing of the past remains? Is it because our pride rose higher than that of all other creatures, and must we alone, like Babel, sink into dishonoured dust?

Behold him thus, this king of the world, this lofty cedar of the mountains; behold man such as the passions have at length made him for us. In his intelligence there was a torch which showed to him, above himself, truth, justice, goodness, the unlimited space of being and its eternal duration: it was reason. Incomprehensible image of divine reason, ours is in us the principle of all comprehension, the point whereby we touch God, in infinitely withdrawing ourselves from the measurable spheres. Reason is man in possession of himself and of God. How can it be extinguished? How can living man suddenly lose consciousness of his spiritual and moral life, even to following no longer the trace of the thoughts which remain to him; like a hunter, from whom the prey escapes which he would still pursue? I know not. God alone knows the place he strikes, the spring he breaks: for us, spectators and victims, we see without understanding and weep without being instructed. Like the proud king who exclaimed: *Is not this the great Babylon, which I have built to be the seat of the kingdom, by the strength of my power, and in the glory of my excellence?** and who, suddenly struck by God, was hurled from his throne, even amongst the beasts of the field, so do we see minds, which but yesterday studied the stars of heaven and the shoals of thought, perish in the opprobrium of madness. Now, the thread of truth is broken for them; memory still presents its materials to them; they listen, they speak, they join words together, but without ideas responding to that connection by their logical agreement, like a palace whose architecture had been broken by a sudden catastrophe, and whose stones, endowed with motion, vainly seek the place they once occupied. Unutterable spectacle of misery! These unhappy beings have not the instinct of the brute, and they have no longer the higher light of man. They would grow greater if they could descend, but they cannot. The human form remains to them with a frightful lowering of its physiognomy, and the gleams of in-

* Daniel iv. 27.

telligence which still wander there add to their fall the tragic character of derision.

I have no need to prove to you that this intellectual leprosy is caused by the disorder of the passions. The science of medicine has proclaimed it loud enough to render it needless to repeat it, and if inheritance sometimes inflicts it upon the innocent, it is an aggravation of a primitive punishment due to the general laws which govern the transmission of life. The passions tend, by their nature, to weaken reason, because they act against its orders and its light; their root is even most living, when they are not altogether corrupt, in a want to extinguish that sacred light *which lighteth every man coming into the world*. Need we wonder that at length, and in certain cases, they obtain their unnatural end, and that reason breaks down under their parricidal efforts? Madness immediately precedes eternal damnation, not in the sense that every ruined intelligence is for ever condemned, but in this sense, that it is the most terrible and the most perfect image of the soul separated from God. Hell will have greater torments, it will not perhaps have any greater degradation.

It is by the amount of madness and suicide that we must judge the moral misery of a people. For, although this punishment is an exception, it is nevertheless proportionate to the number and strength of the passions which agitate the multitude. Pure morals, moderate ambition, strengthen in a people the organs of thought with those of life; the peaceful exaltation of virtue replaces there the intoxications of pride and the agitations of voluptuousness, and if it cannot preserve them from all misfortune, misfortune finds in them at least a temperament capable of resisting it. But when a nation becomes enervated in enjoyments and exults in inordinate desires, its constitution declines rapidly, and at the first blows of fortune we see its children, unaccustomed to struggle and pain, become a prey to distaste for life, or fall under the assault of madness. It is for you, Gentlemen, in casting a look upon your contemporaries, to decide by this rule as to their progress in true civilisation. Perhaps you will find there notable reasons for fear, perhaps also, in presence of these calamities which generations inherit with all the rest, you may complain that God has given you, in the passions, so perilous, not to say so fatal, a gift; you may regret that liberty has not been given to us alone, and that, by its side, a power so pure and so elevated, the passions have established their tumultuous empire. But it would be an unjust complaint, a slavish regret; if you were free without your passions, you would doubtless do good, but you would not love it enough. Passion in man is the sword of love, and he who would snatch it from him because of the evils whose instrument it is, would be like the wretched being who would break the lyre of Homer because Homer sang of the false gods. Ah! break not the lyre! Take it from the hands of the blind poet, and sing with it the name, the blessings, and the glory of the visible God. Sing; earth listens to you, and heaven answers; for the lyre of Homer is also the lyre of David, and the passion that destroys man saved the world on Calvary!

THE MORAL LIFE.

My Lord, Gentlemen,

The end and the obstacle of life are known to us. The end is God; the obstacle the passions. Consequently the whole action of life is henceforth between the end and the obstacle, for life being a movement towards the end, it can only attain the end after overcoming the obstacle by a serious struggle.

The spectacle of life is then, in the present world, the spectacle of this struggle; and liberty, as you have seen, being the adverse power of the passions, it follows that the combat should take place between these, and, in fact, it does so take place.

Here, Gentlemen, in the meeting of these two powers, in their lawful union under the empire of duty, or in their more than civil warfare, since it is the war of the soul against the soul, lies all human history. It is yours, it was that of your forefathers, it will be your children's. Were I to open a soul, and read what passes there, I should read only this; were I to open the annals of the human race, no matter at what page, I should see nothing else there. When the Greeks crossed their sea to land upon the shores of Troy, it was the first famous struggle between liberty and the passions. When the Persians poured in upon the hallowed soil of Greece the numberless battalions of servitude, it was liberty that waited for them on the plains of Marathon and on the waves of Salamis. When Jesus Christ came into the world, it was liberty—the power of good at its highest expression—that came down from heaven to combat upon Calvary, and curb there with a mighty and divine hand the inveterate passions which weighed upon mankind.

Such was the history of your fathers, such is yours. I know not which of these will one day remain master, whether the reign of justice will be established in the world, or whether, on the contrary, evil will triumph; but whatever the supreme result may be, whether justice falls or is victorious here below, I leave its secret and sentence to God, contented, whatever may happen, with having taken a part in the battle which I shall never regret; with having ardently and sincerely followed the banners of liberty and the party of good, remembering, even should we perish, those magnanimous words drawn from a sceptical writer by the omnipotence of truth: "There are triumphant defeats that vie with victories, and the

The Moral Life.

four sister victories, Marathon, Salamis, Platæa, and Mycale, the most glorious that the sun has shone upon, will never dare to oppose their united glory to the defeat of Leonidas at the pass of Thermopylæ."

Whether another Thermopylæ awaits us, whether victory or defeat, let us boldly enter the battle-field, not as idle spectators, but as those whose lot is to be decided before their eyes, and who have a hand in the action which is to destroy or save them. Let us learn in our present hour of combat the tactics which should give us empire—empire at first over ourselves, and, if we are not fortunate enough to share it with others, an empire which will not only be our own over ourselves, but which, even in that narrow limit, will suffice for us before God.

If liberty were alone it would doubtless be vanquished; for, although liberty is the power to act, the very inner spring of our activity, and consequently the principal force; yet passion, notwithstanding its subordinate and passive character, as its name indicates, includes a seduction which becomes a temptation, a poignant seduction, a strong temptation, which naturally has the advantage against a faculty unmoved by it. But, thanks to God, liberty also is not alone; it has an ancestor which combats always with it and for it—that ancestor is light. Liberty, in fact, would not exist if it were not led and sustained by a luminous principle. The inferior being, the animal led by instinct, knows it not; in him instinct and passion are but one and the same thing, and whatever he may do he obeys a fatal impulsion which governs him and keeps him in the sphere where God has placed him. It is not so with man; endowed, it is true, with instinct and passion, inasmuch as he is **united** to a body, and thereby subjected to the yoke of sensible things, **he rises towards God by the light** of reason, and, in that faculty of knowing—so great and so high—he takes his stand against the calls of servitude; his liberty is nourished in the contemplation of the Being, sovereign over all others, and, if he does not lose sight of the earth upon which his members hold him, he mounts at least towards the intelligible orb where omnipotence itself is ruled by a law of justice. It is the view of that law which is the bulwark of our liberty against the assault of the passions.

God, who is the first and infinite activity, has he in his nature anything that directs his will and his actions, or, as an arbitrary ruler of what he wills and what he does, is he immutably seated in the autocracy of an eternal caprice? If God had nothing in him that directs his will and his actions, it is manifest that he would act at hazard, without motives of which he could take account, and consequently without reason. Now, to act without reason is to be in the state of madness, which it is impious and absurd to affirm of God. God, then, who is the highest activity, is also the highest reason. He sees what he does, and why he does it. His light does not limit his power, because the infinite cannot limit the infinite; it penetrates it on every hand, and the immensity of the one is equal or rather allied to the immensity of the other. Every act of divine sovereignty is also an act of divine reason, and this is why Plato desiring to name God called him LOGOS; Cicero, SUMMA RATIO; the Gospel, VERBUM. But what is wanting to this reason which directs God in his actions, and which consequently is his rule, in order that we may call him by a name venerated among us, and yet a strange name when it refers to God—I mean the name of Law? Does God bear in himself his law, a law of which he is no more the author than he is the author of his existence, but which forms part of his uncreated essence, and which, in its reflection upon us and upon things, is the universal source of justice and equity? Do not doubt it, Gentlemen, and in order to understand it, hear St Thomas of Aquinas, who, after Aristotle, gives you the definition of law: *Law*, he says, *is the rule and measure of actions, now reason is the rule and measure of actions, because reason is the first principle of activity in reasonable beings.*[*] Law

[*] 1, 2, Quest. x., Art. 1.

and reason are then one and the same thing, and St Augustine, applying that admirable identity to God, does not hesitate to conclude that *God is eternal law, because he is sovereign reason.** We are far, you see, from that parricidal definition which Justinian gave of law: *Law is what the prince pleases.*† Happily it is not even what is pleasing to God, but what is eternally present to him as just in the immutability of his judgment.

Behold the law which appears to our liberty before the passions which abuse it. Even as divine liberty is held by divine reason, human liberty is enlightened by human reason, or rather created by it, since without it, knowledge, deliberation, and choice would be all wanting to it, and there would remain to man, with the instinct of the animal, only the powerlessness of an activity subject to inclinations alone. Reason creates our liberty by revealing God to us; it directs and sustains it by showing us in God the sacred law which binds God himself to his own reason, and does not permit him to act, were it even towards a grain of dust, without a motive drawn from the contemplation of his own essence, which is at the same time and always truth, justice, and goodness. I say, were it towards a grain of dust, for dust has

---

* "On Free-Will," book i., ch. 6.
† "Digeste," liv. 1, *des Const. du Prince.*

The Moral Life.

its law also in God, the mathematical law, which pre-existed all bodies, and determined in the divine thoughts their nature, force, and action. God could not fail to call them to the reality of being; he could not withdraw from their idea, and in their idea was contained their law. It is that law which governs in space the inanimate worlds that fill it, and the creating will which scattered them when and where it pleased, nevertheless obeyed their very creation, which made of each of them the representation of an eternal and consequently a necessary type. Therefore, even in the movement of the stars or the course of the waves, the law that directs is found side by side with the power that wills, and the harmony of the universe, from one end to the other, is but the resounding of reason in liberty.

If matter itself has its intelligible law in God, how much more intelligent beings! If the relations between beings without spontaneity, without life, without pain or pleasure, are regulated by immutable notions which form a part of the divine understanding, how much more the relations of beings who think, who will, who love, who suffer and who enjoy, who are called in fine by their nature to happiness and perfection! Therefore the law that governs them, the moral law, is as superior to the mathematical law as spirit is to body, as free beings are to slaves. The mathematical law is the law of necessity, the moral law is the law of liberty. It does not draw mechanically, it determines by persuasion; it does not produce a mute and impassible order, but a living order, whose beauty touches the heart because it comes from the heart. God, who is subject to the mathematical law when he creates or maintains bodies, is inwardly foreign thereto of himself, since nothing in him is matter; but the moral law is his own, his reason applied to himself before being applied to intelligent creatures, and in descending from him upon us, it might change its name, but not be for us what it is not for him. There was one law at Athens, and another at Rome; there is but one for humanity and divinity. Therefore, in the Scriptures, God speaks as a being who treats with us and who is bound by his engagements as we are bound by ours. *Men*, said St Paul, *swear by one greater than themselves, and an oath for confirmation is the end of all their controversy. Wherein God, meaning more abundantly to show to the heirs of the promise the immutability of his counsel interposed an oath, that by two immutable things, in which it is impossible for God to lie, we may have the strongest comfort.**

But the moral law not only binds liberty by showing to it its road, and in this road its duty, it is also

* Heb. vi. 16, 17, and 18.

the mother of right; that is to say that, made for free beings, its object is not to enslave them, and that, if it forbids them unjust desires and actions, it also manifests in answering them, the desires and actions which are the inalienable patrimony of the liberty of spirits. The principle and revelation of duty, it is at the same time the principle and revelation of right, and these two terms which constitute it, springing from the same source, being equal to one another, inseparable from one another, pass together from God to man and from generations to generations, distributing throughout the whole intelligent life the balance of its forces, and producing in the midst of the moral world that harmony which I hailed just now in presence of the physical universe, and which I again call, under another point of view, the resounding of reason in liberty.

But reason united to liberty, however great and holy that alliance may be, is it sufficient to guard us against our passions and open to us the road to our last end ? God has not thought so. In fact, notwithstanding the light which the knowledge of the moral law brings to us, there always remains this difference between the passions and liberty, that the passions take their root in our outer and inner sensibility, whilst liberty is a simple force seated in the spiritual centre of our being and naturally inclined by the vehement impulsion which passes from our senses to the imagination and troubles with the course of our blood the depths of our spirit. It was needful that liberty should be succoured where it is attacked, and that something should come to it from the heart to communicate also to it the character and ascendency of a passion. This marvel is wrought, it dwells within us. There where the senses speak, where the imagination vibrates, at the point where intelligence and sensibility meet, a divine essence was one day shed, on the first day of our fall, and since then, the good which was a light and a law, has also become a taste, a sentiment, an attraction, a delight, unspeakable joy when the soul is faithful to it, bitter sadness when the soul betrays it, the gate of heaven, in fine, or the wide threshold of the place of malediction: you recognise conscience. Conscience is reason inspired by love; a sacred wedlock, within the sanctuary of the two most holy things among those which are not God.

Which of us, Gentlemen, all flesh and blood as he is, has not enjoyed in his conscience the chaste intoxications of justice? Which of us, urged by passion, has not at some time preferred his duty, and tasted in the holocaust the unutterable presence of Him who has eternally joined together happiness and perfection? It is in the solitudes of conscience that the most beautiful mysteries of man are enacted. There, injured innocence, oppressed weakness, unmerited misfortune find their refuge; there, fall the pure and avenging tears, and no temple, however holy, no sanctuary, however blessed, is so near to God as the conscience of the just, and above all of the just suffering.

Ah! I begin to breathe! I feared that God had not done enough against our passions, and that, enamoured above all of our liberty, by abandoning it to itself, he had prepared for it too difficult a triumph. I fell into the greatest of all errors, the error of ingratitude. If our passions are many, if there is no place in our flesh and in our soul which they do not hold with their illusions, we have also against them, at every point of our being, a watchful and a sublime guard, liberty, reason, and conscience; liberty at the centre, as force; reason at the summit, as light; conscience between them, as sentiment; all the three closely united, and God behind to sustain them also by the secret influence of his invisible majesty.

Nevertheless, Gentlemen, man remains vulnerable because he remains free. He may, by using his liberty against itself, misuse his reason and betray his conscience. He may abuse his strength, extinguish his light, stifle his remorse, leave nothing remaining in him but broken ruins. It would be his own fault, I grant ; and although I grieve to see such a power of destruction in so feeble a creature, I ask myself if God has not prepared for justice an incorruptible sanctuary upon earth, and if there is not somewhere in favour of conscience, a place of shelter for our infirmity. Ah! it is so, I take refuge there beforehand against myself, and I know that I shall not need to leave humanity in order to remain a man. If I betray my conscience, if Bacon of Verulam, Chancellor of England, betrays the honour of his magistracy, a whole people will rise up to judge him. Justice will spring from the multitude, the tribunal of God will rise up from them in vengeance before outraged Westminster. If the nation itself, formed by servitude for corruption, should in its turn lose the sense of right, it might indeed fall into the tomb never to rise again, but it would not carry with it the conscience of the human race. Other nations, witnesses or instruments of its fall, would be present at its burial, they would see the corpse pass by with scorn, and lawful heirs of its life, because they will have become in its place the representatives of honour, they will sing with faith the symbol of duty, which is also the symbol of immortality. If, in fine, in an evil hour, the whole human race debased ceased to believe in justice in order to think only of interest and pleasure,

The Moral Life. 83

if our eyes should ever behold in the world the abject unity of depravity, ah! believe and do not despair, believe that such a day will be like the day before the resurrection of the Saviour: the human conscience has perhaps eclipses also, but if it has them it has also its Easter, and the age of Christ rose upon the age of Nero.

Yes, conscience reigns. It preceded the Gospel, and will outlive it. It preceded as a dawn, it will outlive it as a sister. The Gospel is the cry of the conscience of God in the conscience of man, and as long as God shall live, as long as man shall not be extinguished, that cry will be stronger to save than the passions are to destroy.

But the passions subsist, and we must combat them if we would overcome them; for God, in arming us against them, did not pretend to release us from peril or effort. He has made us causes. Now every cause should act, and where it meets with an obstacle to its action, it should surmount it by that generous energy which we call labour. This is why labour is the law of life, the law of all creation and all progress, and here we find it again at the entrance of the moral world, as God imposed it upon himself in the seven days wherein he produced and ordered the universe, as he imposed it upon us in remitting to us his work, and in saying to us: DOMINAMINI,— *rule*.* Labour, it is true, was not then what it

* Genesis i. 28.

has become for us. Even as our soul was pure, the earth also was good for us, and we ruled the one and the other with a sceptre which was not heavy. Sin, which has withered all, has not left to labour its primitive character, and God, who had said at the beginning: DOMINAMINI,—*rule as masters*, said in the second age of our destiny: IN SUDORE,—*by the sweat of your brow*. Such is the labour which now fertilises all things. *The field is the world*, said Jesus Christ in speaking of his own; *the field is the soul*, we may say in speaking of ours. But what must be done to our soul? What is that culture which, in spite of the passions, should open to us the road of God, the road of our perfection and our happiness? We are free, and good is known to us, and we possess even the sentiment of it; this is the starting-point: but the passions are there also. They also weigh upon us. They have the advantage of offering to us a present and a seductive object. What must we do in order to sow this field and uproot the tares of the enemy?

I speak in regard to moral life, without yet entering upon the domain of a higher life, and, consequently, I hold only the resources of conscience and reason. Now the first act of reason against evil, is to hinder it. All evil, all passion, has its root in the atmosphere of our life, in the age, people, family, affections and things in which we dwell and which dwell in us. No man is born alone with his body and his spirit; he is the necessary fellow-citizen of a phase of the world, carried along by it in a whirlwind which governs him, and, if he would recover the empire of his personality over himself, he must raise himself by an effort of separation above and beyond his place here below. Like Abraham he must hear that first call of wisdom: *Go forth out of thy country, and from thy kindred, and out of thy father's house.** That is to say, leave that which abases, enchains, and corrupts thee; for the beginning of sovereignty over ourselves is to burst the outer bonds and to find ourselves alone with our own infirmity. But who can thus trace around himself a line of circumvallation? Who can escape from the ideas of his times, the customs of his country, the traditions and friends of his youth, from that phrase in fine of the most profound of historians: *To corrupt and be corrupted, this is called the age.*† None, Gentlemen, none can do this, save the man who has God present to his thought, and who, by him, the father of all ages and the country of all nations, embraces in his soul an horison freed from bondage because it is freed from limit. This is why God, after having told the patriarch to go forth from his natal land, said also to him; *Walk*

---

* Genesis xii. 1. † Tacitus.

before me.* And when the wisdom of antiquity desired to recall its disciples to the inner ways, it engraved that famous sentence: *Know thyself;* not upon the profane pediment of a public building, but upon the threshold of the temple. It is God who is liberty, light, justice, the way, and whosoever does not seek him in his conscience and does not find him in his reason, or whosoever after having known him neglects him as wearisome or rejects him as a burden, is a man lost in the infinite vileness of human inclinations; he may cover his misery by pride, but misery will consume him from within, and death will shake him from the tree like a branch without life.

When man has found God, and chosen him as the polar-star of his moral direction, he is armed. He can pass beyond and oppose to the waves of his passions an act of the will itself, the act of resistance. Resistance is still passive, it is but a refusal. But this refusal is powerful, because it exercises the will, causes it to yield, strengthens it, accustoms it in fine to command, which is its empire. The senses, in their turn, undergo the action of a resistance which is reproduced. Even as the passions trace living furrows there, whose impression upon the soul incites it to evil and weakens it, the will also stamps its orders upon them. It stamps the mark of its sovereignty,

* Genesis xvii. 1.

The Moral Life. 87

and when it returns again, its road is less difficult, because the obstacle is less strong. This progress felt encourages the soul. The soul is warned that the course is clearer, that the imagination grows brighter, that the brain, the centre of all sensations and all movements, gains in solidity and lends itself with more docility to the calm functions of thought. The work of transfiguration appears.

The soul must be aided, however, by something more expressive than resistance, by an act directly opposed to passion. For, in strategy, he who defends himself without attacking loses the half of his forces. The will should, then, when passion demands from it an act of avarice, respond by an act of munificence; when it demands a satisfaction of pride, oppose to it a lesson of modesty. Thus, you descend your staircase to seek your pleasures; on the threshold of the door remorse seizes upon you; you say to yourselves: Go no further; remain at home. This is resistance. But you see a poor man, your heart is moved; the temptation to a good work succeeds to that of a bad action, you open your purse and pour into the fraternal bosom of misfortune the money destined to a guilty distraction. It is more than resistance, it is the movement opposed to the fault, the revolt of the whole soul against the egotism of evil. Now nothing but good is strong enough to destroy evil. Do then all the good that you are able to do, even when it is foreign to the evil that possesses you; for good brings good as gold brings gold. Besiege your passions with it, if I may be allowed so to speak; narrow their circle more and more; sooner or later you will strike them a decisive blow by a last good action.

For there is a term to the moral struggle even here below, a visible reward which is the promise and prelude of the final reward. When the first Brutus descended from the tribunal where he had condemned his sons, and whence he had seen them led to death, he returned to his house, preceded by the consular fasces and the nascent image of the people-king. He sat down at his deserted hearth, near to his silent Lares, and nature overcoming Rome within him, he wept. The gods saw his tears, and they pardoned him, for he had done his work and theirs; he had founded the Roman republic. Thus, when we return from the combat with the passions, mangled and bleeding, but victorious, we may weep before God for what it has cost us; God will not be offended by our tears, for we have founded in the soul of a man more than the Roman republic—we have founded virtue.

Virtue is here below the prize and the term of the combat against the passions. It is the reign of justice in the soul, its acquired and constant conformity to the divine nature. By virtue man attains possession of his whole being. Henceforth he sits in presence of human things as a crowned elder; he sees them from above by a hallowed light, without fear for himself, without indifference towards them; and, if called to take his part therein, he descends to them as the consuls descended from the temple to the capitol, in the majesty of right and the serenity of power. Subject, because he is still man, to the evils of life, he piously receives them from the hand that deals them, thankful in the evil days for those which have been brighter. And, even as sorrow keeps him in the consciousness of his human condition, the thought of a fall, always possible, holds him before God in the fear of a creature who must die and who might fall. It is life without shadow; conscience without trouble; reason without error; liberty without weakness; the fruit ripe, in fine, for the eternity which sowed it. So Jacob appeared when he found again his lost son; so Moses when he saw from the mountain the land promised to his people, and which he was not to enter; so also David, when he advanced with his sling and his youth against him who defied the army of God, or when at the feet of the reproved king he played the harp to console a destiny vanquished by his own. For virtue does not need the help of years; it is born in a day as well as in a century, and whether it shine on the brow of the youth or on the wrinkles of the aged, it is the complete expression of greatness to the people who witness it. Neither Greece, at the summit of its Parthenon, nor Rome, upon its triumphal arches, will ever raise up a more eloquent or more sublime monument, and whatever applause may have adorned the trophies of genius, that which remains on the summit of history, for the honour of man and as a lesson for the future, is the all-powerful and sacred image of virtue.

Virtue is one in its essence. It has for its principle and pattern the eternal law of justice which is in God; for its seat, the human soul; for the secondary cause of its being, liberty, reason, conscience acting in concert; for its end, the voluntary transfiguration of man by his acquired likeness to the divine nature. It is the mediator of earth and heaven, the mediator also of all ages and all generations. It is by virtue that order subsists, by it that respect becomes established and affection flows in the arid veins of the human race. All philosophy that disdains virtue will perish by scorn; every party that rejects it is a party conquered; all friendship without it has no root, and will have no duration; all happiness where it is not will be like a flower that opens at morning and fades at evening; all glory which does not claim it as a sister is tarnished. It is the beauty of time, and the immortality of that which passes away.

The Moral Life.

Like the wisdom of God which penetrates all, it dwells in the cottage of the poor as in the palace of kings, and the unction which it pours into the furrow of the herdsman is as pure as that with which it fills the heart and the chalice of the priest. The child sports with it on rising from his cradle; the youth draws from it the candour of his visage and the tenderness of his look; the mature man asks from it courage, consolation, public esteem; the aged, his last rest; and the world, the secret of its creation.

Although one in its essence, virtue nevertheless multiplies because of the diversity of the objects and acts to which it should be applied, like that seed of the Gospel, the smallest of all, and which became a great tree in whose branches the fowls of the air lodged.

It is this outspreading of virtue which it remains for me to show you to-day. Permit me, Gentlemen, to do this with simplicity and in husbanding my strength; for I need to reserve it for something which I would say to you in concluding, and, if possible, in a manner so that it may never be effaced from your mind.

The ancients decided, and we have not altered their decision, that there exist four fundamental virtues to which all the others return as to their natural trunk. We call them cardinal virtues, and we still range them, from respect for logic as much as consideration for antiquity, in the same order in which they placed them. The first is prudence. It is at the beginning of all the others, because it embraces human things in their most general point of view. We are, in fact, depositories of a portion of the universal life, and, as God governs all life, we govern, under him, that part which has been confided to us. We are what the Roman language expresses by the word REX,—*king*, that is to say, rulers and magistrates of life. Not our own only, even this would be much; but our life blending with that of our contemporaries, that of our contemporaries with the life of their posterity. It is true that we wield a sceptre whose influence extends far beyond us. We are not princes of the earth, rulers of states, nor princes of thought, governing the mind of men—this is but for the few; but we are all, however lowly our condition, princes of life, because we rule it, or, to use a more common expression, but which is a still higher one, we are a providence. We have received from God that admirable faculty of foreseeing and providing, which, in an infinite order, constitutes divine Providence itself. We foresee the future, and, in the future, the effect of our actions; we dispose them for an end, we remove possible obstacles; in fine, we form destiny, that terrible thing which we often accuse of fatality, and which is but the consequence of our own decisions. For if it be granted to us to foresee and to provide, it is not always permitted to us, or rather, it is hardly ever permitted to us, to withdraw completely from the universal drama a fault which we have cast into it. Having once left us, it advances, it is borne along by the course of things, it takes its place in the general movement, and in forming our condition it forms also the condition of many.

In vain then should we desire to limit the field of our life to ourselves, and reduce prudence to a kind of egotistical virtue, useful at most to ensure us peace and quiet. Prudence is a royal virtue. When Philip counselled the Athenians, if my classical memory does not deceive me, to trouble themselves less about his views and projects, the Athenians answered: "We take account not only of the affairs of Athens, but of the whole world." So is it with each of us. Wittingly or unwittingly we throw our dice into the course of life. And, if you still doubt it, what, I ask you, is it that forms the destiny of the human race, if not that of nations? And what forms the destiny of nations, if not that of families? And who form the destiny of families, if not the father and mother, that is to say, you? All holds together, all is linked together in the moral, as in the physical world, and the difference between the two is only on this point, that the one has necessary beings for its agents, the other free beings. But liberty is not the incoherence of actions and the inconsequence of results; liberty, being an order, has its laws. It produces a regular web, in which the times are interwoven under the hand of prudence, in which the past commands the present, and the present invites the future.

Justice comes after prudence to forbid whatever is unjust, that is to say, whatever is against the right of a man. But what is the right of a man? Man is entire in his life, and his life is entire in the lawful object to which it tends, which is God, and, by the possession of God, perfection and happiness. Perfection and happiness in God—this is the first right, the absolute right of man; for necessarily every being has a right to the end which God has given to him as the motor and term of his life. But, even upon this earth, man is on the road to his perfection and happiness; he aspires to them, he labours for them, and if he does not enjoy them, he has at least in his heart and in visible created things faint lineaments of them. If God is the end, the world is the road; and, inseparable from his right to eternity, man draws therefrom his right in time. Crowned upon the other shore, he is thereby crowned also upon this. It belongs to him to live there, and consequently to

The Moral Life. 95

draw therefrom the elements of his life, that is to say, of his perfection and happiness, and none can deprive him thereof without injustice. But, if the right of time be the same in itself for man, as the right of eternity, there is this difference between them, that in God, who is infinite, the right of the one can never be an obstacle to the right of the other; whilst here below, because of the narrow limits of this world, it inevitably happens that the perfection and happiness of these may be adverse to the perfection and happiness of those. Whence it follows that the secondary right of man, his right of time, should not be expressed in an absolute manner, but under a restrictive form, which, in protecting man, will also protect mankind. In a word, duty must temper right, and man must respect the perfection and happiness of all, if he desires that all should respect his perfection and happiness. This is the true right of time, the right which is human although it is personal, and which carries with it the peace or war of the world, according as it is interpreted by egotism or by virtue.

The upright man, the honest man, is he who measures his right by his duty. He knows that man, an infinite being by his destiny, is cast transiently upon a limited soil, and, unable to enlarge the common country, he enlarges his heart in order to content himself with little. He cleaves to the seat of life, and, rich or poor, whether he gives or receives, he prepares for himself a tomb where none will accuse his passage of having been a misfortune. Ah, Gentlemen, I am a Christian, and yet I am moved by that name of honest man. I picture to myself the venerable image of a man who has not cumbered the earth, whose heart has never known injustice, and whose hand has never executed it; who not only has respected the goods, the life, the honour of his fellow-creatures, but also their moral perfection; who has kept his word, been faithful to his friends, sincere and firm in his convictions, proof against time which changes and would include all in its inconstancy, alike removed from obstinacy in error, and from that special insolence of apostacy which marks the baseness of treason or the shameful fickleness of inconstancy: in fine, Aristides in antiquity, L'Hopital in modern times. Behold the honest man. When you meet him, Gentlemen, I do not ask you to bend the knee, for he is not yet a hero, but he is already a noble thing, and perhaps, alas! a rare thing, at least in its plenitude. Salute him then as he passes, and whatsoever you may be, a Christian or even a Saint, love to hear in your ears, and above all in the depths of your conscience, that beautiful word: You are an honest man.

Temperance is the third cardinal virtue. It is moderation in desires and wants, especially in what concerns the life of the senses; food, sleep, movement, repose, outer pleasures. By temperance, man limits himself to what is good for him; he makes of his body a being obedient to the truth of his nature, obedient also to the law of justice. For all that we retrench from what is unprofitable or excessive turns to the profit of those who have received less than ourselves; and, without this scrupulous measure in the use of things, it is not possible to render to others all that is due to them.

Thus, the prudence of the magistrate, the justice of the honest man, the temperance of the sage, these are the first virtues, and as it were the first lines which constitute moral rectitude. This done, much is done; nevertheless this is not yet enough; moral rectitude exists, moral greatness is absent, the man is worthy of esteem but not of admiration. Now he should merit admiration, because he is the son of God, who is admirable in himself and who has willed to be admirable in his works, the chief of which is man. And, virtue being the highest thing in man, there should be in it, besides prudence, justice, and temperance, which do not suffice to his greatness, another virtue, a supreme virtue which gives to him the majesty of what is august, the splendour of character, and bends the knee of mankind touched at having produced in itself such great representatives of itself.

Have you ever noticed the feeling produced within you by those ancient peoples whose history we studied in our youth? We were not taught, and accustomed, to study the Persians, the Indians, or the Chinese, all those eastern races, the oldest of all perhaps, and whom, on account even of their antiquity, some have vainly endeavoured to bring upon the living scene of our age. The peoples with whom we have lived from our childhood, putting aside the predestined nation which held the deposit of all the truths and all the promises of God, those peoples, our old masters and our old friends, were, and still are, the Greeks and the Romans. Why, Gentlemen? Why these, and not others? What all-powerful charm makes them still our teachers, and places their books in the sacred hands that hold open the Gospel before the world regenerated? Perhaps you have thought that the cause of this lies in the beauty of their literature and art. And it is true that they have divinely written, spoken, sculptured their glory and their thoughts; marvellous workmen of the intelligence, perfect models of taste, who may perhaps be equalled, but who will probably never be surpassed, and of whom it will always be true to say with Horace—

GRAIIS INGENIUM, GRAIIS DEDIT ORE ROTUNDO
MUSA LOQUI.

The Moral Life.

But this is only the surface or the first page of our admiration for them. There is a deeper cause, of which I would speak as I feel, and for which I have hitherto husbanded my voice and my strength.

Learn then, and pardon me this emphasis, learn that not justice only has been commanded to us, that not only has it been said to us: Thou shalt respect right; but that right, justice, good, truth, all the divine things have been entrusted to us as their guardians and avengers. Learn that we are here below the pretorian guard of justice, the sword of right, the sanctuary that contains and the army that protects them; for they have enemies, never doubt it, immortal enemies; all those who hate what restrains them, all blasphemers against order, because order condemns them, heavy battalions which genius sometimes leads, which even sovereignty does not always disdain to keep in its pay, and which, for six thousand years, hold God in check and mankind in peril. Justice is but a doctrine, and all doctrine has behind it a wide and deep pit ready to bury it; what saves it is the blood that it may give to fill it. Now, this blood is ours. And, in order to give it, to pour it out in streams in the present and possible occasions when justice may have need of it, we must have in our hearts another virtue than prudence, temperance, and justice itself; we must have that last virtue which crowns the others by raising them to the dignity of martyrdom, the virtue which Rome called force—FORTITUDO, and the Greeks by the very name of Rome; for Rome, in the Greek language, signifies strength; a prophetic name given by Providence to that city which it had destined to govern the world by the empire of right and the empire of character.

For think you that Rome reigned by the steel of her legions, and that Greece conquered Asia with the lance and buckler? If you thought so, you would not possess the first idea of man or the first idea of God. Rome subjected the world, Greece conquered Asia, by virtues. Whilst the other human races, bent under a settled servitude, passed obscurely through time, the genius of public life awakened on the Greek soil and on the banks of the Tiber. Speech created opinion, and opinion gave birth to the responsibility of all before the conscience of all, power became a magistracy; laws, an expression of the natural relations between men; obedience, respect for order; glory, an ornament to the country; liberty, a right and a sentiment, the right of self-government, and the sentiment of personal dignity. This new life—of which Moses on Sinai laid the foundations in the soul of another people, the elder brother of Athens and Rome—produced virtues unknown to the East. It made of man a citizen, that is to say a public man, and conscience increasing with duty, morals became strengthened, characters formed, heroism developed, and a cry of admiration rose up from the world towards posterity, which still listens, and will never weary of listening to it. Descended from the heights of Horeb, in presence of the first people withdrawn from servitude, it was repeated from the fields of Attica to the summits of Latium, linking between them in the same immortality the names of the Maccabees and the Scipios, the memory of David, and the remembrance of Philopœmen. A sublime gathering of all that was great, a sacred council of all the mighty souls and actions, in which our childhood lived, to which Christianity without fear or without jealousy has led for their instruction the generations entrusted to its care, and from which it has presented them from age to age, under a thrice holy shield, to the events and sacrifices of redeemed mankind. There, were formed the new nations which Clovis and Theodoricus established upon the ruins of the old world, and which Charlemagne one day united under the triple majesty of religion, war, and letters. There, sprang up chivalry, the open flower of human sentiments purified in divine faith; and thence it carried back the cross to the tomb of the

Saviour. There, the ages in which we live were prepared, ages of painful struggles, greater than any before them had yet been, but wherein, on solemn occasions, heroism has not been wanting to any cause worthy of inspiring it. Thus from Moses to us, in a course of three thousand years, history has found the same virtues which produced it. The contemporary of free nations and Christian nations, it has lived by their glory, and, in perpetuating it, has called forth the admiration which makes its own immortality.

But where lies the action of this moral force sprung from physical force? What is its impulsion? Destined to make us bear our misfortunes bravely, and to arm us with constancy in favour of justice, is there somewhere in us a point which may be called its natural seat or the foundation that sustains it? Gentlemen, there is a line which I believe to be celebrated, so familiar is it to me, and which never fails, when it comes back to my memory, to cause me sadness which I can hardly overcome. When Orestes, wandering upon the shores of Taurida, found himself unexpectedly in presence of a sister whom he loved and whom he had lost, at the moment of his unlooked-for happiness these doleful words escaped from him:—

> "Day by day man learns to despise life."

It is a great expression, and its accent is deep. It is not, however, the true expression; it touches, it moves, but it depresses us. It is a cry of weakness, and not of virtue. The true expression should have been :—

> Day by day man learns to despise death.

Contempt of death is the principle of moral force. As long as the conviction of justice does not reach this point; as long as there is a fear of death, as if to die were any other thing than living and attaining to God, there is nothing to hope for from a man on great occasions. A threat is sufficient to vanquish him; he will float on listlessly as events bear him along, and should history know him it will know only his shame. It is contempt of death that makes the soldier, that creates the citizen, that gives to the magistrate his toga, to the prince his safeguard in perils and his majesty in misfortune. Charles I., King of England, had known many weaknesses, and an error, by separating his throne from the traditions of the country, at length placed him defenceless in the hands of his enemies. In the eyes of the multitude it was an irremediable abasement. But when the monarch, vanquished and prisoner, entered the hall where his accusers, become his judges, were seated; he appeared there so calm and with so much authority, that respect covered his person with a return of his greatness, and although powerless to regain his throne and to save his life, he was able at least to die with the certainty that he died as a king. History, like him, has believed it, and his statue, standing at Whitehall, still moves the posterity who behold it, and who admire, in so great a misfortune, so magnificent an effect of greatness of heart.

Young men, I turn towards you. It is an old habit which you must forgive in me. I have so often called you to the road of great things, that it is difficult for me to keep your remembrance and your name from my words. You have a long career before you; but if you prefer life to justice, if the thought of death troubles you, that career, which you paint so brightly, will sooner or later be darkened by weaknesses unworthy of you. Citizens, magistrates, soldiers, a time will come for you when contempt of death is the sole source of good in word or action, when private virtues no longer shelter man, but when it is needful to possess the fearlessness of a soul which looks above this world, and which has placed there its life with its faith. If that faith be wanting to you, in vain will your country count upon you, in vain will truth and justice look down upon you from heaven, their eternal abode; and in vain will Providence bring under your feet events capable of immortalising your life. You will not understand them. Glory will pass before you, offer you its hand, and you will be powerless even to call it by its name.

But what is glory? Times are greatly changed since it had altars. The future of truth, of the universal expansion of justice in the world, is henceforth the question amongst us. Christianity has opened ways to us which antiquity knew not; all is enlarged —right, duty, responsibility, man, and the world. Consequently higher virtues are required, greater sacrifices, and more virile souls. When the three hundred Spartans awaited the innumerable hordes of effeminate barbarism at Thermopylæ, they knew well that they must die, and one of them, desiring to leave an epitaph upon the tomb of his fellow-soldiers, with the point of his spear cut upon the rock that famous inscription: *Passer, tell Sparta that we died here to obey her holy laws*. This, from whatever point of earth or heaven it may be seen, is an heroic spectacle, and the Christian ages have not refused to it their admiration. But they had nearer to them another Thermopylæ, a Thermopylæ bathed with purer and more plenteous blood. Like Greece, Christianity has had its barbarians to conquer, and the narrow passes of the Catacombs were the Thermopylæ where its faithful ones saved it by their death. Surely they also might have graven upon the rock an inscription worthy of their martyrdom, and it would not have been: *Tell Sparta*, but, *Tell the human race, that we died to obey the holy laws of God !* But He for whom they died had taught them that modesty of which ancient heroism knew nothing.   They died then without pomp, unknown to Greece and to themselves, and when at length glory sought them underground, it found but their blood.

Here, Gentlemen, you will perhaps stop me, you ask me where is the happiness whose name charmed your ear at the commencement of this discourse, as the object of your life and the final end of man? We have come to blood, to martyrdom, to sacrifices under the most austere form: is not this a strange road? Strange, if you will, but I do not swerve from it. In the glorious path where the course of ideas has led us, I feel like you the thorns which threaten or wound my flesh; they are sharp, they form a road of which you may say all, save that it is not the road of heroes and saints, the road of all those who have honoured their nature, immortalised their life, served their brethren, and respected God.

THE INFLUENCE OF THE MORAL
LIFE IN LEADING MAN
TO HIS END.

MY LORD, GENTLEMEN,

We now know the three terms of the mystery of life; the end, which is happiness and perfection in God; the obstacle, the passions; virtue, the means of surmounting them, and at the same time the reward of the empire we may have obtained over them. It is of virtue that I spoke to you in our last conference. I showed you that it flowed from liberty, reason, conscience, and the labour of man; and next, how it spread out in four branches, called: prudence, justice, temperance, and force.

This done, Gentlemen, we are still far from having reached the term to which our faculties tend, that is to say, to God, our beatitude and our perfection. For although it be true that passion may be overcome by virtue, and thus the obstacle which arrests us on the road is removed, nevertheless, it does not follow that we have reached the threshold and possession of our destiny. We must advance another step, we must seek whether virtue really leads a man to his end; in other words, whether it is an efficacious principle of beatification and deification.

This, as you see, is a supreme question. For being

certain that there are within us only two sources of activity, namely, passion and virtue; being certain on the other hand that passion withdraws us from the true road of life, and consequently from its end, as we have shown, and as is but too evident: if virtue itself were powerless to lead us thereto, it is manifest that we should no longer have a future before us, but a mystery without issue and a fatality without solution.

Is it so? Is this the conclusion we must draw from ourselves? And is mankind divided between a despicable herd which seeks in the abjection of vice an illusion which will not even be granted to them, and certain men also deceived in a contrary road, and obtaining from virtue only apparent greatness in real inanity? You do not think so; the same instinct which causes you to love virtue causes you to believe that it is not sterile, but that it contains the germ of a transformation which begins in us here below, and by prophetic signs forebodes its reward beyond this life.

Here below, do I say? Did I not, in the beginning of these discoursess, in rendering justice to the generous ideas of the stoics, blame them for having made virtue its own reward and for calling themselves happy because they thought themselves virtuous? It is true, Gentlemen; nor is it my intention to maintain that virtue gives happiness here below and becomes confounded with it, but that it prepares and even distributes it in a certain recognisable measure, as also it forms within us an outline of the divine nature which will hereafter be communicated to us in the plenitude of an incomprehensible effusion. Virtue, in effect, cannot be the road to God without bringing us nearer to him, and it cannot bring us nearer to him without our receiving from that presence which increases, a life and foretastes of a higher order. There should be in the virtuous soul something which is not found in the corrupt soul, something which is not virtue alone but its rebound upon all the faculties of our being, and which, in purifying them, in elevating them, should produce satisfaction and beauty; satisfaction which is the germ of happiness, beauty which is the reflection of God.

I was twenty years old, when, for the first time, from the heights of the upper Jura, I saw at my feet the tranquil waves of the lake of Geneva. It was towards evening. The summit of the Alps glowed in the last rays of light, and threw them back upon the lake in soft shadow. The silence was pure like the air and the water, and it seemed as if nature, before giving us the repose of night, had herself become calm in holy meditation. For a long while I watched that beautiful vision, the imperfect image however of the human soul when virtue has brought to it peace. *Peace*, says St Augustine, *is the tranquillity of order*. As long as the passions govern us, they produce a confused trouble within us, which makes of our life a succession of contending and painful emotions. The joy which we seek in them becomes changed into a fever which dejects and exalts us, turn by turn, without ever giving us repose in contentment. But, as soon as virtue dawns upon the soul, it produces a first calming of our faculties. The imagination, which represents to us and magnifies the things of the body, retires before the intelligence, whose purified vision better contemplates the immoveable heights of the invisible world; memory, instead of raising up noxious shadows before us, begins to respect the modesty of our desires; the senses themselves, touched by fear, are less prompt to rouse against us their insatiable appetite, and the whole being, bent before reason, takes the submissive attitude of a creature which knows its duties, and, in accepting them, obeys its own royalty. When that state continues, it becomes peace. Peace is not complete joy; it is but calm joy. It may be that some shade of sadness still dares to approach the tranquil shores of our life; but that sadness, because it is a passion, encounters in virtue a force which restrains it, and the veil with which it covers our feelings and actions is never a shroud, still less is it the frenzied trouble of despair. The virtuous man knows how to suffer; he knows that suffering is in the world, and that, as a child of the world, he should bear his part in it, and neither reject nor curse it. He does not, like the Stoic, say to pain: Thou art but a name; but he says to it: I know thee, thou art my trial, my merit, doubtless also my expiation, and thou wilt one day be my crown. Should fortune knock at his door, he is alike unmoved. Content with little, he receives what is beyond it as a gift which was not needed; and, greater than any elevation given to him, stronger than any power that comes from without, even upon the throne he preserves the peace of modesty in the glory of simplicity.

Peace ! I have said that is not complete joy; still less is it happiness. But if anything, however, precedes happiness among us, if this supreme good has, like our temples, a porch, a mysterious shade as a guard and a precursor, ah ! peace, doubtless, is that shade, that porch, that something unspeakable and sacred, which is neither God, nor his sanctuary, but which gives to the soul a pious presentiment of them. The sage may be deprived of his happiness because he may be deprived of the things which he loves and which he has a right to love ; but his peace is beyond the power of any one. It is in him like himself, the effect, the reward of his virtue, the effect of a free cause, and which a free act alone can withdraw from him. Like the virtue from which it springs, peace is stamped with the seal of liberty, and this seal, which is within, cannot be broken by any strange hand, how powerful soever it may be. As no tyranny is able to deprive a man of his virtue, so none is able to destroy his peace. This is why Jesus Christ, raised from the dead and leaving to his own his passion and death, nevertheless said to them in an infallible promise: *Peace I leave with you.* He did not say to them, I leave with you happiness. It would have been too much and too soon; but without fearing for their martyrdom, he said to them: *Peace I leave with you.* A sublime expression which has created the tranquillity of all the saints, and which has left souls standing upon the ruins of so many things and of so many ages.

The Stoics rightly understood that virtue should produce something marvellous in man, but they did not know what, and confounding that which invincibly belongs to the liberty of man with that which is foreign thereto, they declared that the sage is happy, instead of simply declaring that he is in peace whatsoever may happen to him. Their view was penetrating, but it passed beyond the limit of truth, the limit which the Saviour of the world has defined by that ineffaceable expression:—*Peace I leave with you.*

It may be supposed that peace is a kind of heroic indifference, and that in proportion as the soul becomes master of itself it loses the spring of sensibility. This is not true. The sage suffers in his soul as in his body. He pities, he regrets, he hopes, he weeps. But he does not abdicate his sovereignty over himself, and the waves of life, although reaching him, break upon a certain point where nothing yields. So far from virtue abating or repressing sensibility, its second privilege is to touch the heart and open there the source of affections. It is commonly supposed to be passion that loves, because love readily begins by sympathy wherein liberty has no part. But this first movement of love is not love. In the main, all passion is but egotism. It flies indeed to the sympathetic object, but only to devour it. Its end is voluptuousness of the senses or voluptuousness of pride. Now what is either of these but a personal enjoyment in which we immolate another to ourselves? Pride would subject the universe to itself in order to make of it the stepping-stone to an elevation which has no rival; the senses covet every object which they meet with in order to make of them their instrument and their victim. There is nothing there but blood hidden under famous names. True affection springs from virtue. It is virtue alone that inclines us towards a being not to satisfy our appetites but to communicate to them our good. Sympathy remains. I do not deny that it is, as it were, the basement of love, its cause and its germ, a germ sometimes deceptive, and which ends only in debauch, weariness and faithlessness, as long as virtue does not intervene to inspire sacrifice, and give to love by sacrifice its generous and immortal form.

Love has then this particular character, that it is a passion in its root, and the masterpiece of virtue in its essence and its summit. It corrupts all when it remains a simple passion. It saves, it regenerates, it elevates all, when it becomes a virtue. The ancient, like the modern world, knew love; but in the ancient world it was too often only a passion; in the modern world it is a virtue. Filial piety and maternal piety, conjugal tenderness, friendship, patriotism, all these sentiments which are the honour of man, have drawn from Christianity strength and purity which they did not before possess, because as virtue increased love increased with it.

Now love is, with peace, a manifest element of happiness. To love is to live by the heart, by the most active and consolatory part of our being, where personality quits its solitude and is moved by a presence which is not its own; there where we may be two without ceasing to be one, where tears are garnered, sufferings divined, faults forgiven, and where even pain, because it is borne for another who is dear to us, assumes a sweetness which is not without its pleasure. And when peace comes to join with love, when there dwell together in the same soul that which moves and that which calms, that holy alliance forms an unction which is not happiness, since so many things are necessary in order to be happy, but which is, as it were, its smile and its first perfume.

However, these two great blessings, peace and affection, are not the term where ceases the efficacy of virtue acting upon the soul and creating its reign therein. It brings to man, under a still greater name, a good which is not less necessary to him than the two first, namely: glory. Do not suppose that glory is a movement of pride, whereby we take pleasure in ourselves, and joyfully contemplate those beneath us who have not reached the same height. Do not believe it; for the Gospel, which commands us to be *humble in heart*, commands us also to be certain that glory, and an eternal glory, is the reward of virtue. And St Paul, speaking to the first Christians already persecuted, hated, mocked at, nevertheless said to them: GLORIA NOSTRA—*Our glory*. The Christians had a glory in the catacombs and upon the scaffolds, the true glory, that which popular favour neither gives nor takes away at will, and of which no power can despoil the human soul which has conquered it by meriting it. *Our glory*, continued St Paul, *is the testimony of our conscience.** Conscience tells the good man that he is great before God, because he is pure before him, and that greatness sustains without elating him, because, being founded upon truth, it remounts to God much more than it descends to man. The soul feels its dignity, and rejoices therein. It feels that it is unalterable, and yet dependent upon virtue, which is its principle, and which itself depends upon the liberty come from God and aided by him. That glance cast at the same time upon our excellence and its cause keeps us in a state of grave dignity, which fills without dazzling us, unlike that false glory which does not come from justice, but from the favour of the people or events, and which, clothing us in false purple, exalts us the more as it is the less merited.

The glory of virtue, Gentlemen, is not within us only, it leaves the soul and spreads out around the man. However lowly and obscure he may be, a man has parents, friends, a city, and, sooner or later, his actions will be judged, he will find around him the esteem which God grants to us, and of which our conscience is the sure guarantee. In vain does hypocrisy cover itself with a veil, or fortune surround us with its illusions; there is in mankind a sentiment of good

* 2 C or. i. 12.

and honour which never deceives it. Even the throne does not shelter princes from this judgment. Domitian reigns, but Tacitus writes. And it is one of the most admirable arrangements of this world that no empire and no success has been able to subject history, and impose upon posterity by its means. Generations of kings sprung from the same race have followed each other during ten centuries in the government of the same people, and, notwithstanding that perpetuity of interest and rule, they have not been able to hide from the world the faults of their fathers, and maintain upon their tomb the false splendour of their life. History, one day or another, under the unknown pen of a contemporary, or under the tardy pen of a man of genius, unveils their heart and chastises their memory. The triumphs of Alexander do not defend him against the murder of Clitus, and the tranquil death of Sylla no longer insults the blood of his victims. Virtue alone continues its reign throughout ages, and neither tyrants nor falsehood can arrest the stream that bears it on to the admiration of the world.

There is in this glory of conscience a feature which might not appear to you, and which I must draw forth from its shade, or rather from its light, in order that you may remark it. The sentiment which good, performed under the eye of God, gives to us, includes a certainty which elevates and consoles us above all things—the certainty that our life is useful, and that it does not pass in vain in the world. Lost as we are in the visible and invisible immensity of things, overwhelmed by the spectacle of earth and heaven, prospectives of history and boundless horizons of the future, we cannot arrive at the conviction of our littleness; our soul protests against our eyes; from the abyss wherein it seems to be thrown and overcome, it suggests to us the thought that we serve, and the invincible desire to serve in reality. I do not speak of the common utility, although that is even noble, of founding or perpetuating a family, of creating a patrimony for posterity, of upholding and honouring one's country, of leaving, in fine, an honoured name to one's family. This is already a great deal; but it is not enough for our soul. Time is a limit which causes it to fear for its works, and the ruins accumulated in the course of ages tell it too plainly the vanity of so hazardous a service. When the consuls observed the Capitol, the Temple of Jupiter appeared above the destinies of the Republic, and, however dear Rome was to them, whatever place she held in their hearts, they heard a mysterious voice that demanded more of them, and foreboded something higher. What we need, in order to feel our usefulness and attach us to our life, is the certainty of working for something eternal; and this we have. We have it by virtue. Labourers in a work begun by God, we bring to it a stone which ages will never shake; and, how feeble soever may be our part in the common edifice, it will be there for eternity. Thus, in the days of the middle ages, Christians were seen to quit their country in order to devote themselves to a cathedral rising on the banks of a foreign stream; satisfied with their day, because it had been useful, they observed, in the evening, how much the work had risen towards God; and when, after twenty or thirty years of obscure labour, the cross shone on the summit of the sanctuary built up by their hands, they cast a last look upon it, and, with their children and their remembrances, they went away, without leaving their name, to die in peace, in the blessed thought of having done something for God.

The Gospel has said of Christ: PERTRANSIIT BENEFACIENDO—*He went about doing good.* It is a short expression of a whole life, but it suffices for those who understand it, and the heart knows nothing sweeter than when it can apply it to itself.

Nevertheless, whilst enumerating the fruits which virtue produces in the soul, a fear seizes upon me. Man is not all soul; he has a body, the organ and companion of his life, the child of God like the soul itself, and this body, called as it is to immortality, has, during its sojourn here below, wants which neither peace, nor love, nor glory can satisfy. Will virtue come to its help? Will virtue nourish, will virtue sustain it? Oh, virtue, holy stem of all the good that dies not, thou hast given me peace, thou hast given it to me to love, thou hast given it to me to live usefully and honourably in my conscience; but I have a body inseparable from me, a body poor, naked, corruptible, which demands from me its daily bread; wilt thou give it? Canst thou pity earthly miseries? Or, insensible towards such evils as unworthy of thee, dost thou disdain to provide against them?

Gentlemen, all the laws of the world are in harmony with each other, and if virtue be useful to the soul, it is also undoubtedly useful to the body. *I have been young*, said David, *and am now old; and I have not seen the just forsaken, nor his seed seeking bread.** The honest, sober, and industrious man earns his bread. It is the general order, and a little experience of life suffices to prove it. All inability of existence amounts to some virtue outraged, whether of justice or temperance, prudence or force, and, if unforeseen accidents may be justly accused thereof, they are but exceptions to a rule too evident to be mistaken. Virtue nourishes the soul, and the soul

* Ps. xxxvi. 25.

nourishes its body. You think, perhaps, that it does not do so grandly? This I grant, for the more the soul becomes elevated, and tastes delight in God, the less the body needs; the progressive lessening of the wants of the body is even one of the most infallible signs of virtue; and the sages of paganism, in disdaining riches, spoke beforehand the language of the Gospel, and prophesied in their way that expression which opens the new law: *Blessed are the poor!* Therefore God, who has profusely dealt out spiritual gifts to us, and who has placed no limit to peace, love, glory, an infinite treasury from which all may take at will, God has appeared sparing of the goods of the body. He has measured out bread and water to us with a parsimony which would be terrible if the reason thereof were not what I have just said, and if there were not in abundance a vivacious principle of corruption. Would it have been just to reward virtue by giving to it opportunities of falling? The human race is then poor, it will always be poor, because true riches is in virtue.

I have just named the human race, and this name warns me that in considering the efficacy of virtue in the soul, I did not open to my thoughts a field sufficiently vast. The soul, in fact, is never alone, and, in order to know it entirely, it must be seen in the state of a people. A people is an assemblage of men united by the force of the same ideas and the same sentiments, that is to say, by their soul. Doubtless the community of territory, interests, and laws, plays a part in their association, but this part is not the first, because the body and earth hold in nothing the first place when man is in question. A people amongst whom souls are not united may preserve the outward appearances of a people, but in reality it has ceased to be, and an accident sooner or later will cast it among the number of nations that are no more. It is here, then, where the soul and its works appear in their full revelation; and, if it be true that virtue engenders peace, affection, glory, the immortal utility of accomplished good, something of all these things will shine forth on the brow of a virtuous people, with the majesty which adds to the greatest, number and duration. Now, who can deny this, and what do you find in history? What have those nations been upon earth which have left an honourable trace behind them, those amongst whom devotedness has made citizens, or peril has created soldiers, or long designs, firmly developed, have directed the events of the world and marked their place on the tables of Providence? What nations have been great in their life, what nations have remained great after their death? And if there are alternatives of elevation and abasement in history, if reverses follow prosperity, if death follows life, what is the sign which announces to generations these turns of fortune, these comings or these disappearings? You know, Gentlemen, and I have no need to tell you: when Scipio was chaste, Rome destroyed Carthage; when Rome was corrupt, Cæsar reigned there. For, as it has been forbidden to history to betray virtue by hiding the truth from us, so has it been forbidden to nations to be free as soon as they have ceased to be virtuous.

Behold then, viewed in the secret of the soul or by the light of ages, the action of virtue upon our destiny. Whilst vice, as I have shown you, produces within us, as its natural effect, sadness, despair, suicide, madness; virtue engenders there peace which strengthens and consoles, an effusion of pure and sincere affections, a glory which neither seeks nor fears the eye of man; and, if I do not dare to call all these blessings by the perfect name of happiness, at least they form its dawn, and, as it were, its first outline. They foretell for us what they do not yet give to us, and the weakness which may remain in them is a proof to us that God alone is able to complete in us the work that virtue begins.

But God can be our happiness only inasmuch as we possess Him, and we can possess Him only inasmuch as we are partakers of His nature; for it is impossible for two beings who have nothing in common in their nature to penetrate each other to the point of possession one by another. If we are in the true, if virtue is really the way that leads us to God, it must then have in itself an efficacious principle of deification, that is to say, a principle which transforms our being in such a manner that it becomes capable of beholding God, and of uniting itself to Him.

Now virtue, such as we have presented it to you, is not a perfection of a negative order, which simply retrenches excesses, or which fashions the soul in lines circumscribed by time and space. No, Gentlemen, virtue communicates to us, makes intimate and personal to us, things which have the infinite for its sphere and eternity for its seat. It gives truth to our intelligence, justice to our will, goodness to our heart, and consequently the same mode of thought, will, and feeling as God himself, who is by His essence truth, justice, and goodness. If our being is finite in its substance, if it is also finite in its faculties and its functions, it has at least that prerogative of knowing the true, of willing the just, and of loving the good, three things which are not itself, which are not included in the narrow limit of its existence, from which it is able to separate itself by an act of its liberty, but which it is also able, by another act of the same empire, to invoke and retain to itself.

There lies the point by which its nature is susceptible of that enlargement and transformation which theology does not fear to call deifical, since that truth which it is capable of seeing, that justice which it is capable of doing, that goodness which it is susceptible of loving, what is it but God? Therefore, because of the root by which our nature plunges into the divine abyss, Scripture declares upon its first page that man was *created in the image and likeness of God*.

Perhaps I should not have dared to say this if the word which never deceives did not come to the help of reason, and I might have halted before the thought, that no likeness can be conceived between two beings one of which is infinite and the other finite; but that is an illusion of terrestrial optics. When we observe two material lines, one of which is supposed to be unending, the other limited, they seem to us to bear no proportion to one another, because one does not act upon the other and derives nothing from it. Between God and man, on the contrary, there is intercourse at the point of truth, justice, and goodness. Man sees no truth which is not in God as his thought, consequently as his essence, nothing being in God in the state of accident. Hence, by this fact alone, which can be denied only by atheism, man, all feeble and limited as he is, holds relations with the infinite. He does not contain it, he does not measure it, but he receives its light with liberty, as his eye receives in its orbit the effusion of the sun which enlightens all the heavens. We must admit this, or else submit to one of these two negations: either that truth is nothing, or that God is not truth.

But, you may say, if God and man see the same truth, perform the same justice, and give their heart to the same goodness, God always does this in an infinite, and man in a finite manner, and this destroys all likeness between them. All likeness of greatness, yes; all likeness of nature, no. Moreover, what hinders you, by an act of your free will, from willing all the justice that God wills, and loving all the good that he loves? Do we not say to him every day, in the most simple, although the most divine, of all prayers, *Thy will be done upon earth as it is in heaven?* Earth, that is to say, man, is then capable of doing here below the will of God as it is done in heaven; he is able to say to his Father, What thou willest, I will; what thou lovest, I love. And if not by the intelligence, at least by the will, he thus establishes a kind of equation between God and man. It is the privilege of the will, being free, to extend its horizons at pleasure, and to will even beyond what the understanding clearly conceives.

Whatever man may do, there always remains to him, by the institution of his nature, the germ of the divine likeness. But this germ becomes impaired and corrupted by vice, that is to say, by the domination of the body over the soul, of the animal over the spirit. The animal is not capable of anything divine; he feels and tastes only what is body or has some relation with body; his sight, his touch, his instinct, all his faculties, whatever name may be given to them, do not go beyond this. And, when man, descending from the heights of the soul by corrupting himself, condemns himself to bear the yoke of animality, he soon loses sight of the regions which are natural to him, the infinite no longer appears to him save as an abstraction of the mind, as the unreal void wherein move the things tangible to sight and touch; his science lies altogether in the knowledge of outward phenomena, and, if mathematics are still prized by him, they owe it to the side by which they touch bodies, and not to the side by which they touch the real infinite, which is God. Justice declines for him in the same proportion: it is no longer in his conscience a law that creates duty there, a light that reveals to him the eternal order of beings endowed with life and liberty; he sees there only a calculation by means of which interest may be preserved. Even goodness, that last treasure of the soul, survives there only in the degree at which we remark it in the animal, under the form of instinct and the empire of sensation. A sad shipwreck where man perishes, not because he is immortal, but where his nature sinks so much the more as it subsists and reproaches itself for its own unworthiness.

It is there that the breath of virtue seizes man and uplifts him, or, if he be not fallen, it is there that it keeps him from falling and becoming lost. Man owes to it, then, intact or restored, the salvation of his nature, he owes to it to think, to will, and to love in a divine manner, to be, in fine, according to the expression of St Paul, *the offspring of God.**

Now the likeness of nature brings with it a likeness of beauty; for beauty is but the physiognomy of beings in all their splendour, and there, where beings resemble one another by the fount of their nature, they necessarily resemble one another by their physiognomy. Man has, then, a likeness of physiognomy with God, and consequently, a likeness of beauty. We do not see it altogether, it is true, because of the veils which the body throws over our souls; nevertheless, in spite of that obstacle, something of it transpires upon our outer visage, upon our forehead, in our eyes, our lips, our smile, and all that

* Acts xvii. 28.

expression which the hidden flame of our faculties and the obscure perfume of our virtues manifest outwardly. It is impossible for a soul to retain within all the light of its thought; a light will rise in spite of it, even to the furrows which the thoughtful habits of the mind stamp upon our flesh. Nor can it any more hinder justice, or temperance, or force from giving us somewhere a sign of their presence. The form grows under the repeated concussions of great actions, and the nobleness of secret inspirations is revealed by traces which command inevitable respect. Still more powerless is the soul against the sensible effusions of goodness. Goodness being the highest gift, because it is in God the aroma of the infinite, has received, in coming to us, a special grace of manifestation; all indicates the benevolent heart to our view; its silence even has an eloquence that attracts; it touches without speaking, it pleases unconsciously, it reigns by an empire which costs it nothing, and which none other would be able to equal. The whole soul thus rises of itself to the surface of the body; it vivifies its features and gives a character to them which nothing in the rest of nature resembles, because nothing in the rest of nature, how magnificent soever it may be, has a direct relation with the visage of God. That of man alone is its shadow. I do not even use a sufficiently strong expression, and I must borrow the inspired language of David in order to say how human beauty is an image of divine beauty. David then, beholding it with the certainty and the rapture of a prophet, suddenly exclaims in one of his psalms: *The light of thy countenance, O Lord, is signed upon us*—SIGNATUM EST SUPER NOS LUMEN VULTUS TUI, DOMINE!* It is the divine light, and not its shadow, that is signed upon the face of man, because that face expresses truth, justice, goodness, three things which are the fount of the essence of God, and whose radiation forms the eternal splendour of His physiognomy. There is but one truth, and that shines forth in our look; there is but one justice, and that appears upon our brow; there is but one goodness, and that inspires our lips; there is but one beauty, and it shines forth from the east to the west of our being like a dawn which rises distant, and gilds, in awakening, the tranquil summit of the heights that it contemplates. The virtue of man upon the visage of man, is not God as we shall one day see Him, but it is the obscure and living prophecy of His beauty something more than that which Moses saw when God said to him on Sinai: *Look, and thou shalt see my back parts.**

The likeness of beauty engenders sympathy. All

* Psalm iv. 7.   * Exod. xxxiii. 23.

beings are attracted to one another by their beauty; and the beauty of man being analogous to that of God, it follows that God attracts man and that man attracts God. It is by this point that all creation mounts towards its author, and that he himself bears his work with him in the eternal solicitude of his paternity. But, virtue alone giving to man his beauty of birth and predestination, it is virtue alone that maintains between God and him that attraction which springs from a common nature, expressed by a common beauty.

Thereby you see, Gentlemen, that there are in virtue three elements of deification, or, if you prefer it, of positive and efficacious union with God: likeness of nature; likeness of beauty; and sympathy which rises from one to the other.

But is this all the progress of the soul towards God by virtue? Is there nothing between them beyond aspirations of sympathy, and, in calling to each other from the opposite extremities of the universe, do they not answer each other like an echo of time in eternity and of eternity in time? Is it needful that death should intervene in order to advance further, or, even from here below, do we pass into the sanctuary as rewarded pilgrims, and with our trembling hands touch the very heart where lies the goodness which has made us? Ah! I am sure that the hope of it is not vain; I believe in it before having thought of it, or rather, like a man come from a distant and marvellous country, I bring you the account of what I have seen, the all-powerful remembrance of what I still behold.

When I spoke to you of virtue, and named to you its famous divisions, prudence, justice, temperance, force, did you not remark that they all related to man, and that, whilst taking their origin in God, they did not, in their application, pass over the frontiers of humanity? What then! Is there no virtue then whose object is God? Is it that, all having in him their beginning and their end, none tend to him by a direct movement? This is not possible. All beings have a law of their relations, and every law entailing a moral obligation for the intelligence which knows it and the liberty which submits to it, we must say, either that there are no relations between God and man, or that these relations, determined by a law, give to God rights over men, to men duties towards God, and consequently impose upon us a virtue which directly concerns God. That atheism denies this, I easily conceive, it does not admit the notion of the infinite real and living; but, for the man who respects God in his conscience, after having acknowledged him in his mind, it is impossible to believe himself without relations with God, consequently

in Leading Man to his End. 135

without a law of these relations, a law which entails with it duties to perform, and virtue, which is the result of their fulfilment.

But what is this virtue which we have not yet named? What is there more vast than prudence, more holy than justice, more noble than temperance, more magnificent than moral force? When these things are in the heart of man is he not like God? Has he not the reflection of His beauty upon his brow? And whence would he draw forth a better unction or a feeling more capable of enrapturing him? Ah! Gentlemen, I am moved like you before that part of our soul, and I scrutinise it, trembling before that which I seek there, and which perhaps I shall not find.

Tell me, however, do you not think that as God is the most perfect of all beings, we owe also to him what is most perfect in us; that being the infinite extremity of all things, we owe to him the extreme result of our faculties, and what I shall call the masterpiece of man? Yes, I do not deceive myself; if something in us is worthy of God, it must be the supreme act of our life, that something which, in every being, holds the summit of his nature and of his activity. Oh! what is then in us that blessed summit? What is then the masterpiece of man? Homer wrote the Iliad. Is the Iliad the masterpiece of man? Dante wrote the Divine Comedy. Is the Divine Comedy the masterpiece of man? The Romans made the people-king. Is the people-king the masterpiece of man? You smile, and you are right; the Iliad, the Divine Comedy, the people-king, were great things, and their rays still light up the highest summits of humanity. Nevertheless the masterpiece of man is elsewhere. I am sure of it. Where then is it?

If I say to a man, I esteem you; can I not still say something more to him? Yes, for I can easily say to him, I admire you. If I say to a man, I admire you, can I not still say something more to him? Yes, for I can say to him, I venerate you. If I say to a man, I venerate you, can I not still say something more to him? Have I altogether exhausted human language in that expression? No. I have still something left to say to him, one thing only, the last of all; I can say to him, I love you. Ten thousand words precede that word, but none come after it in any language, and, when it has been once spoken to a man, there is but one resource left, namely, to repeat it to him for ever. The mouth of man can say no more, because his heart can say no more. Love is the supreme act of the soul and the masterpiece of man. His intelligence is there, since he must know in order to love; his will, since he must be content; his liberty, since he must choose; his passions, since he must desire, hope, fear, feel sadness and joy; his virtue, since he must persevere, sometimes die, and be devoted always.

Therefore it is written that in God, in the mystery of his triple personality, it is love which comes last and closes the infinite. Love terminates God, if it be permitted to use such an expression, and it is love also that terminates man. I do not hesitate to pronounce its name in this sanctuary, at the very door of the tabernacle where the divine majesty reposes, for, if love has profaners who abuse its name, it has saints who form its guard, and prevent the slightest breath from touching, in order to tarnish, its immortal chastity.

Love being then the supreme act of the soul and the masterpiece of man, what we owe to God is to love him. The love of God is the virtue which we have not yet named, which crowns all the other virtues and opens to us in the way of transformation the issue nearest to the end. For the peculiar quality of love is to unite those who love one another, to blend their thoughts, their desires, their sentiments, all the expressions and all the blessings of their life, and to penetrate even to the substance of the loved one, in order to cleave to it with a force as invincible as it is ardent. Even when love seizes upon limited beings it draws from them a degree of energy which enlarges man beyond himself; what must it be when it takes possession of God? There it finds and gives to us all that is wanting to our feeble nature, it finds God, and it gives us God. Already resembling him by a likeness of nature and a likeness of beauty, already borne towards him by the sympathy which springs from likeness, our love seizes him and clasps him in an ecstasy which will afterwards become complete in the midst of vision, but which, here below, is a prelude of the eternal embrace in which our life will be consummated.

Having reached here the height of the mystery, I am like a man who has long been climbing a steep and high mountain, and who, at last standing upon a solitary rock, sees at his feet the road he has travelled over, and the abyss which surrounds him on all sides. My head turns, I ask myself if what I have said to you is not a dream of my thought, if virtue exists upon earth, if the heart of man is really capable of the prudence which embraces the interests of mankind; of the justice which renders to each what is due to him in the order of sensible good and of the good of the soul; of the temperance which subjects the body to the law of the spirit; of the force which gives even its life for right and truth. I ask myself if there are men who seek God as the term of their passing existence, as the certain principle of their happiness and perfection. I ask, above all, if there are men who love God. I do not say as we love men, but as we love the most lowly creatures, a horse, a dog, the air, water, light, and heat. I ask myself these things, myself first, and then you, and I wait for my answer and yours with the terror which must decide my life. I hear bold voices which tell me that virtue is but a name. I hear from one end of history to the other the protestation of sceptics, the sarcasm of egotists, the laugh of debauchees, the joy of fortunes acquired by the sweat and blood of others, the plaintive cry of hearts which hope no longer; and alone, from the height of these reasonings which have led me to the idea of the true, the good, the just, the holy; steadfastly regarding what I call my soul and what I again call God; I await an answer which will cast me down or confirm me for ever. Who will speak it to me?

I will give this answer to you. You seek the just, the strong, the holy man; the man who loves God. I know him, and I will tell you his name.

Eighteen hundred years ago Nero reigned in the world. Inheritor of the crimes which had preceded him upon the throne, he resolved to surpass them, and thereby to make for himself, in the memory of Rome, a name which none of his successors should be able to equal. He did this. One day a man was brought to him in his palace who was laden with chains and whom he desired to see. This man was a foreigner. Rome had not nurtured him, and Greece ignored his cradle. Nevertheless, interrogated by the emperor, he answered like a Roman, but like a Roman of another race than that of Fabius and Scipio, with graver liberty, higher simplicity, something open and yet profound, which astonished Cæsar. On hearing him, the courtiers spoke softly, and the ruins of the orator's tribune moved in the silence of the Forum. Since then the chains of that man are broken; he has passed through the world. Athens received him, and convoked the remains of the Porch and the Academy to meet him; Egypt saw him pass before its temples disdaining to consult their wisdom; the East knew him, and all the seas have borne him. He came to sit upon the strand of Armorica, after having wandered in the forests of Gaul; and the shores of Great Britain welcomed him as an expected guest. When the ships of the West, weary of the barriers of the Atlantic, opened out new roads towards new worlds, he was there as soon as they, as if no land, no stream, no mountain, no desert, should escape from the ardour of his course and the power of his speech; for he spoke, and the same liberty which he displayed before *in Leading Man to his End.*

the enslaved Capitol he manifested in face of the whole world.

Traveller also to the mystery of life, I have met this man. He bore upon his brow the scars of martyrdom; but neither the blood shed, nor the course of ages, had taken from him youth of body and virginity of soul. I saw him; I loved him. He spoke to me of virtue, and I believed in his own. He spoke to me of God, and I believed in his word. His spirit brought to me light, peace, affection, honour, and that foretaste of immortality which detached me from myself; and, in fine, I knew in loving that man that we can love God, and that He was indeed loved. I offered my hand to my benefactor, and I asked his name. He answered me as he had answered Cæsar: "I am a Christian!"

THE SUPERNATURAL LIFE.

My Lord, Gentlemen,

In following man upon the road of God and of his destiny, we have met the Christian. I have declared that the Christian alone possesses the plenitude of the moral virtues, that he alone above all has the privilege of loving God, and consequently, of being in relations with him worthy of God and of man. Is this true? And, if it be true, how is the Christian here below the only intelligent creature who is in the state in which he ought to be? Is the Christian more than a man? If he be more than a man, how has he reached that superhuman elevation? If he be but a man, how is it that he alone possesses and practices virtues inaccessible to the rest of mankind? These, Gentlemen, are grave questions, upon which we must now enter.

Is it true that the Christian alone possesses the plenitude of the moral virtues? That he alone has known and realised here below the love of God? In order to learn this, we must not consider man fallen below himself, but take him sincerely at the height of his known greatness; for, as it would be unjust, in order to appreciate Christianity, to observe the Christian who is so only in name, it would also be unjust to oppose to the true Christian a man unworthy to appear as the representative of humanity. Let us then observe the true man, the total man, if it be permitted to use this expression, and, neglecting in his history that which is his lesser part, let us seize him, in the authentic course of his annals, at the highest summit where virtue has placed him.

We hesitate no longer. There are nations in the world which, by the special care of Providence, have raised themselves, during a period of the human age, to a glory which keeps them still standing before posterity, and draws from us, in their praise, as if they were our only ancestors, the venerable and singular title of *ancients*. Elect nations even in their territory, they inhabited those two famous promontories so admirably traced by the hand of God, Greece and Italy. A pure sky, in shedding streams of light upon them, spared them however from a degree of heat which would have enervated them; and, holding the middle of the world between the pole and the equator, on the borders of a sea wide enough to open roads to them, too narrow to separate them from the rest of the world, they owed to that predestined position a temperament in which harmony predominated. Art, taste, eloquence, the sentiment

The Supernatural Life. 147

of the beautiful under all its forms, made a part of the Greek nature, and, if Rome, less fortunate, imitated more than she created, she possessed however, like her elder sister, the language which subjugates and the style which does not perish. But that which lifted the one and the other to the summits of history, was that in the servitude wherein the human race was silenced, the one and the other had the instinct of right, and founded, after Moses, without being inspired like him, the second and the third city. As Jerusalem had been founded upon the tables of Sinai, Athens and Rome were founded upon other tables, less sacred, doubtless, since the hand of God had not written them, but which formed nations capable of vanquishing themselves and worthy to govern themselves.

Assuredly, Gentlemen, in taking these as the highest type of human nature, I obey history, and respect truth?

Now what were the virtues of these peoples? It cannot be denied that they possessed prudence and force; prudence, which made them, in their government, the founders of civil liberty; force, which enabled them to defend their institutions against the jealousy of all their neighbours, and ended by giving them the empire of the world. But were they just? Were they chaste? Did they love God? I shall surprise no one by refusing all these virtues to them. For, if they had the instinct and even the science of right, it was in the narrow limits of the community in favour of a small number of men honoured with the title of citizens, and served by a multitude who had no place in their esteem or name in their law. Mankind did not exist for them, and justice accuses them so much the more as they knew and practised it in the egotistical horizon wherein they shut up their conscience. It will always be said that they produced great citizens, never that they respected in man his rights and his dignity. Whence came this ignorance or this scorn of man? How is it that nations whose liberty was so dear to them sacrificed it so willingly in the son of the slave and in the vanquished? It is not now the time to answer this; it suffices to declare it.

The same contradiction is found in them in the order of temperance and morals. By a prodigious exception, they knew before the gospel the unity of marriage, and had thus the honour of placing the family upon its true foundation. But do not ask from them flesh subject to spirit, continency which respects age, the domestic hearth, or even the majesty of their gods; they knew that modesty is the veil of all virtues, but this veil was withdrawn from their hearts, and history sees them as they were, dissolute in their feasts and even in their temples, corrupting private life by the institutions of public life, and leaving to us remembrances which force even our admiration to close its eyes.

As to the virtue which strengthens and preserves all the others, they had doubtless, in their best days, a living religion, and Rome could boast, by the mouth of her greatest orators, of having had equals in war, but not in piety. They brought to the gods, of whatever name, the sanctity of their laws as well as the success of their arms, and the worship of country was inseparable for them from the worship of their founding divinities. Never were they so proud as to believe that reason alone founds and maintains a community, and, still better than a modern historian has said it, they considered that *every nation is a ship whose anchors are cast in heaven.*[*] But if such was their faith, and in order to express it they found ceremonies in which fear and veneration were manifest, they did not however go so far as to foresee the last word of man for God and of God for man; which is love. They believed, they prayed, they trembled, they adored, it was a great deal: it may be maintained, according to St Paul, that they had knowledge of the true God, of the one and holy God whom the regenerated eye of man now contemplates; but they

[*] Rivarol.

did not love him. No trace of this intimate and sweet movement which brings back the creature to his source is found in their books or their monuments. In this, as in morals, as in right, they knew more than they wrought, being greater by the intelligence than by the heart, and presenting to us the spectacle of incomprehensible infirmity in admirable perfection.

And a thing worthy of study, as often as a man even now, ceases to be a Christian or refuses so to be, he falls back to the state of those famous people who preceded the Christian era. He may be Spartan, Athenian, or Roman, but he will neither be just, nor chaste, nor love God. I say that he will not even be just, and for proof of this you have but to observe him in his relations with the poor. What the slave was in former times, the poor man is now. The poor man is the slave emancipated and protected by the law of God; and by what the modern man is towards the one, you see what he would have been towards the other. Now, has the man who is not a Christian any affectionate feeling towards the poor man? Does he treat him as a brother? Has he any idea of his dignity, any serious concern for his soul and his body? I shall not venture to say that philanthropy has no action upon every heart closed against the Gospel; but if there are examples of benevolence inspired by reason alone, I admire them as generous exceptions,

The Supernatural Life. 151

and this rarity proves to me that they are not the effect of a cause capable of generally producing it. You may perhaps say that charity should not be confounded with justice, and that the absence of the first is not a convincing proof that it is a stranger to the second. It is true that charity has another name than justice in human tongues, and even another meaning. But in divine language, the one is not without the other, and he alone is just who loves man for God and with God. It is this love that Christianity has brought into the world, and which is at the same time its work, its title, and its privilege. The Christian is a man who loves God; man is an intelligence who does not love God.

How is this? How is it that the ancients, enlightened by so bright a light and capable of such exalted virtues, halted at the limit where their history shows them? How is it that the moderns, still more enlightened, and sprung, however they may act, from more generous blood than that of heroes—the blood of saints, lose all the fruit of their race as soon as they separate from Christianity by the apostasy of the mind or the heart? Manifestly, the ancients had no idea of humanity; and this it is that rendered their justice so imperfect; but they had the idea of country, and it is this that made their great citizens, that is to say men capable of two-fold strength—

strength to live under regulated liberty, and strength to die in its defence. The Christian, preserving the tradition of country, because it is honourable and just, has heard a word greater than that of the Forum, and he has believed in that word which said to him: *There is neither Jew nor Greek; there is neither bond nor free; there is neither male nor female; for you are all one.** The ancients did not ignore that they had a soul, and even they believed that it was immortal. But its true value was imperfectly known to them. The Christian learned it all in that second word: *What doth it profit a man, if he gain the whole world, and suffer the loss of his own soul?*† The ancients perceived God by the light of their reason, and under the shadows of false divinities; but that God, too much hidden, touched their hearts only by fear and hope, and their blood never arose with that of sacrifice towards the invisible majesty which held them in suspense. The Christian has learned the last word of God in that third expression: *Thou shalt love the Lord thy God with all thy heart, with all thy soul and with all thy mind!* Thus, to the virtues of the ancient succeeded the virtues of the new man; to the straightened and oppressive community of Greece or Rome, the society of mankind; to the purely civil and political life, the spiritual life; to the reign of

* Galat. iii. 28. † St Matt. xvi. 26.

The Supernatural Life. 153

great projects, the reign of God and souls; to the times of glory, those of charity.

But, once more, how is this? How is it that the ancient man could not attain to the life of the new man? Is that transformation due to the slow and natural progress of ages? Is the Christian only a Greek or a Roman a few years older; an intelligence ripened by the work of ages?

If we consult history it will show us Christianity suddenly overflowing, like an unforeseen wave, upon a degenerate civilisation, and springing neither from the anterior culture of great peoples, their laws, their morals, their reason, nor their religion; but falling upon them with sudden light and violent empire, although feeble and persecuted. Far from having prepared and conceived that state of life, the ancient world, in accepting it, fell beneath its weight, and generations, strangers to all intellectual tradition, all regulated order, formed the starting-point and foundation of another moral universe. If the Christian life were a simple progress of mankind, it is evident that it would of itself become perpetuated in the midst of nations civilised by Christianity. Now, it is not so, as we have said. As soon as the modern man abdicates his Christian faith he falls at once under the imperfection of the past; he remains more instructed than Athens, but not more chaste; as strong as Rome, but not more just; as sage as the Lyceum or the Academy, but, like them, no longer knowing enough of God to love him. Even this is perhaps too much to grant to the pride of apostasy, and it would be more true to maintain that the unbelieving Christian is not even comparable to the man of ancient times, because the man of ancient times had a faith and he has none.

Gentlemen, every phenomenon has a cause, and every cause is proportionate to the phenomenon which it produces. Since then the Christian life is a life manifestly superior to all others; it has necessarily a principle from which it derives its being, its power, and its perpetuity. What is this principle? In order to understand it we must learn what is, in general, a principle of life.

God, who is life subsisting in itself, without origin and without end, is the first principle of all life. But, by a design worthy of his greatness and goodness, he has willed to communicate to his creatures, in order to give them greater likeness to himself, something intimate and fertile as the transmissible germ of their own life. All life, then, in every degree, pre-exists in a germ, and the germ differs according to the perfection of the life which it contains. One thing is the germ of the plant, another of the animal, another of man; and this germ, whatsoever it may be, determines and limits the life which springs from it. In material beings, it is but a form capable of developing itself by a movement of growth, an elementary principle of simple vegetation. This is not yet the true life, because it is wanting in spontaniety, that is to say, in the sentiment and possession of itself. But as soon as life manifests itself by spontaneity, the germ itself changes its nature; it rises, it passes through matter, it becomes, under the name of instinct, a principle of vision and of impulsion; of vision, for the being can only move spontaneously towards its end or its object by possessing in itself at least an initial knowledge; of impulsion, for it does not suffice to see in order to act, it is necessary also to be attracted towards the term of action. It is thus that the animal sees exterior nature by its senses, and is moved towards it by its wants. The germ or the principle of its life is no longer a simple form destined to be developed under the inevitable empire of air, light, and heat, but something active in itself, a substance superior to matter, and which is the first degree of spirit. Doubtless it is not the spirit that makes the body of the animal, but it is the spirit that enlightens and moves it.

In man, in whom not only spontaneity is manifested but liberty, who has not only nature but God for end, the principle of life proportionately increases; he becomes a soul, that is to say, a spirit capable of knowing in mathematics the law of bodies; in logic, the law of thoughts: in morals, the law of volitions; and, beyond these laws, Him who is their unchangeable source and their eternal seat, namely: God. It is to this point that we have followed man in our former discourses; it is there that we find him again; it is there, above all, that we must not halt, since a life higher than human life has been revealed to us in the Christian, and since that life, like all the others, must have a principle capable of producing and explaining it. What is it then? What is there beyond a mind that knows God, and what can come into our soul that is higher than reason and more efficacious than liberty?

What may come there, Gentlemen, what even ought to come there, is, in fact, a principle of vision which is above reason; a principle of action which is above liberty; a light which, without destroying reason, perfects it; a power which, without attacking liberty, strengthens it. Christians do not deceive themselves. They recognise in themselves, as the primordial source of their life, a supernatural or divine element which they call grace, that is to say the highest of all gifts, and they all say with St Paul: GRATIA DEI SUM ID QUOD SUM, *by the grace of God I am what I am,** and every principle of life, whatso-

* 1 Cor. xv. 10.

ever it may be, being a principle of vision and impulsion, it follows that grace communicates to him who receives it a vision which nature ignores, a movement whose secret is unknown to it.

But what is this vision, what is this movement? Before grace and without grace man knows God; what more can he see? Before grace and without grace he tends towards God; what can he seek beyond? It is God who is the life of his soul, who enlightens him coming into the world, who receives him on departing from the world, who is, we have said, his beginning and his end; it is by the notion of God in the understanding, by the action of God on the conscience, that man is an intelligent, free, moral being, made in the image of his author, and having in him his beatitude and perfection. What, after this, remains there to raise him higher? And, how divine soever grace may be, how supernatural soever it may be called, is it able to show us more, and give us more, than God?

Yes, Gentlemen, it is able to show us more than God, such as reason shows him to us; and it is able to give us more than God, such as moral virtue causes us to love and merit him.

How do we see God in the light of reason? We see him by our ideas. In regarding itself, the intelligence does not perceive itself as a vague light in an ill-defined horizon, but under the form of precise notions, like those stars that people the firmament, and whose splendour brings to us, with the revelation of their spheres, that of the immensity which contains them. Our soul appears to us enlightened by torches which live, and by the immortal light which shines forth from them behind the ideas of cause, truth, justice, goodness, unity, eternity, infinity, under a veil impenetrable and splendid, we discern the first being from whom our own depends, the inner sun which has no shadow and counts no days. But that knowledge, how sublime soever it may be, is but an ideal knowledge; God does not therein manifest himself directly to us; his person and his substance remain inaccessible to us; and, in being certain of him, certain of his presence and his action in the universe, there remains to us the incomparable disquiet of never having seen him. Now the object of grace, its proper effect, is to prepare us one day to see God, and even to see him here below.

What! see God, see him here below! Yes, and I do not retract that expression, I confirm it, I confess to you ingenuously and without metaphor that I see God absolutely as I see you; and, if you do not believe this on my simple affirmation, I will prove it to you.

Assuredly, Gentlemen, it is your soul that makes

you men, and assuredly also I do not see your soul. Nevertheless, in spite of my powerlessness to see your soul, and so to penetrate the very depth of your being, there where humanity rises and separates you from the brute, you will not question that I see you. I see you as you are, animal and spirit; animal by a body which falls under the investigation of my senses; spirit by a substance hidden from my vision, but which, however, reveals itself to me and manifests to me your true personality. It is by personality that you appear to me in your total nature, that I seize and possess you efficaciously, and even if in the distant obscurity of your soul you willed to withdraw yourself from me, you would not be permitted to escape. I hold you as a person, and that is enough for me; for the person is the real and living reflection of the whole being, and that which characterises it in distinguishing it from all other, and, where personality is visible, the invisible even is unveiled.

But how does the personality appear? How can man, who is soul and body, visible by the one, invisible by the other, and whose distinctive character lies precisely in that close union of two such diverse substances, how can he present to our eyes the mystery of his personality? This is the question. If I saw only the body, I should not see the man; if I saw the soul, a spirit would fall under the investigation of my senses, which is impossible. It is necessary then that through the shadows of the body the soul should make its way, and appear to the eyes of the most simple by unmistakable signs. Now this is what takes place, and that in virtue even of the alliance established by the creator between the two elements which form our personality. The soul which is the principle of our life, penetrates the body, dwells in it, enlightens it, moves it, and, without being able to show itself in its essence, shows itself in effects, the first of which is language. You stand up before me; you are free to be silent and so to hide from me what you are; but beware, if your lips open even but once, it is enough. Whatsoever you may say, there will be an accent in your speech which will not deceive me. I shall read therein, in traces which will never be effaced, first your intelligence, next its degree, the weakness or energy of your conception, the power of your will, your character and your heart. All will appear to me. Language is the living expression of the soul; it springs therefrom as water springs from its source, and it is as impossible for you to disguise it as to change your person into another. Terrible and gentle instrument of the communication of spirits, language, which is their revelation, is also their glory and their chastisement. It reveals man

The Supernatural Life. 161

and judges him; it betrays without avowal even the conscience itself.

What would it be were the conscience to open and declare what it is? Then language becomes not only an expression, a light which shines from within to without; it takes the stranger and brings him within, even to the domestic hearth, there where the soul lies alone and undisturbed in its commune with itself; we become there more than spectators, more than witnesses, we become guests; and confidence, that dear secret of friendship, displays to us without shame the invisible beauty of spirit.

Therefore language once spoken should never die. Come from heaven to be the organ and representation of things unseen, it must hold to eternity, and all fleeting as it is in its nature, become fused as in indestructible brass. Writing has produced this marvel. The written word is the image of the spoken word, as the spoken word is the image of the word thought, as the word thought is the image of the soul that thinks and writes it. That fleeting sound, which comes from your bosom, will perish no more, it is seized at its entry into the world by an art as divine as itself, and which will transmit to generations the living form of your heart. For, Gentlemen, all is written, every word has its book, and that which is not written upon earth by the hands of men is written in heaven by the hands of angels. Every day, at every instant, the inexorable burin of divine justice gathers up the breath of your lips, and engraves it for your glory or your shame upon the tables of immortality.

But language, however expressive and self-revealing, is nevertheless not the last term of our outer apparition. Man not only speaks, he acts. God has cast him into an age, in the midst of events linked with all the past and the future of the world, and, how little soever he may be, he has there his place, his power, and his responsibility. He must decide for good or for evil, for this is the question of all times, and his choice, manifested in his actions, will say for ever to heaven and earth all that he was inwardly. Actions bring to the light of day the motives and mainsprings of the soul, its instincts, passions, ideas, faculties, all greatness and all meanness together; they are to sight what language is to hearing, and, like language, they have a writing which perpetuates them, and which is history. Every soul makes its history at the same time that it makes its book; and from the one to the other, from the history and the book, from the actions and language, results a third and last revelation of ourselves, which is physiognomy.

Man cannot speak and act without all his features

following the movement of his life and being deeply affected thereby. The light of his intelligence passes into his eyes; his brow dilates under the empire of thought; his heart impels the blood to his cheeks, and bends the curves of his mouth into a smile. Shame, joy, fear, anger, sadness, all the virtues and the vices, have each somewhere their chosen place, and, in unceasingly returning to the same furrows by the same action, they leave there the trace of their passage in that stable and moving expression which we call physiognomy. Physiognomy is the painting of the soul, its permanent reflection in the flesh which it inhabits and vivifies. By physiognomy we betray ourselves against our will, and our most hidden life follows us everywhere to our shame or honour.

It is thus, Gentlemen, that the wise Artisan who has made us has known how to bind together the two substances of which he has woven our being, and to manifest that which is not seen by that which is seen. The soul remains hidden in its essence, but it constantly shows itself by the language which it inspires, the actions which it leads, the physiognomy which it animates or extinguishes, and our personality, although characterised by something incomprehensible in itself, is however the most palpable and ordinary of the phenomena of our life. What was needed then in order that God, profiting by that economy founded by his wisdom, should emerge from the inaccessible abyss which hides him from us, and appear to us like ourselves? What was needed in order that he might be seen as I see you, as clearly and as indubitably? One thing sufficed, Gentlemen, and that you divine, it sufficed that, assuming our nature, he should reveal himself in his word, his actions, and his physiognomy; now this is what God has done. God became man that he might be seen, not in his essence, but in his personality; and that personality, sovereign, infinite, perfect, is the constant and lucid object of the vision of the Christian. What the universe is for the eye of man, Jesus Christ is for the eye of the Christian; and, the same as man recognises in the universe the action and the providence of God, the Christian recognises in Jesus Christ the word, the actions, the physiognomy, and consequently the person of God. *That which we have heard*—said St John—*which we have seen with our eyes, which we have looked upon and our hands have handled of the Word of life, this we declare unto you; for the life was manifested, and we have seen, and do bear witness, and declare unto you the life eternal, which was with the Father, and hath appeared to us.**

* Ephesians i. 1, 2, 3.

The Christian deceives himself, do you say? he takes a human word for a divine word; limited actions, and a limited physiognomy for the actions and physiognomy of the infinite; his vision is but a dream, and his life but an error. You say this, Gentlemen—if, however, I may be permitted to impute this language to 'you, you say this; but the Christian says the contrary, and, his life being superior to yours, I believe him rather than you. For it is the life that attests the degree of truth which is in a being, because it is the degree of truth which makes in a being the degree of life; and thus I believe in the animal rather than the plant; in man rather than the animal; and, among men, I believe in him who overcomes his passions, rather than in him who obeys them; in the hero rather than in the coward; in the Christian who affirms his faith rather than in the unbeliever who denies it. I declare, moreover, and I have already told you, that hearing the word of Jesus Christ in the Gospel, seeing his actions and his physiognomy under the relief of Scripture, it is not possible for reason alone to recognise God there. Reason does not go beyond ideas, and although ideas lead it even to God, they only reveal his existence and his attributes, without revealing to it his person. There must be another light superadded to reason, in order that both together, inseparable-

and convergent, may raise man to the vision of the divine personality, and prepare man one day to behold Him in the impenetrable light of the uncreated essence; grace, we have said, is that higher light which perfects reason by becoming united to it, and Jesus Christ, God and man, is the object of grace, inasmuch as grace is an element of vision.

But vision is only the half of life, impulsion is its second part, and in order to understand the supernatural life in its plenitude, we must know the impulsion which man receives from it, and which accomplishes the Christian.

Truth is the fount of every being, and therefore, when we see a being, we necessarily see some truth, that is to say phenomena, laws, a substance hidden under the laws and the phenomena, a connection of causes and effects, a whole, in fine, which unites itself to the universe, and, by the universe, to God. But truth, how deep and vast soever it may be in the being wherein we contemplate it, is not however that which first strikes us, nor is it that which most powerfully attracts to it the observation of the mind. Truth has a vesture, a halo, something which touches our inmost feeling, and against which we cannot shield ourselves save by a supreme effort of virtue; it is beauty. Whilst truth alone leaves us masters of ourselves, beauty moves us; it attracts and enraptures us, it subjugates us even to leaving to our liberty, only that which God, by his omnipotence, maintains there against all seduction. Truth halts at the intelligence, beauty penetrates even to the heart; it is, in all beings endowed with knowledge and feeling, the first motor which gives impulsion to them. Whilst truth arrests us within ourselves to consider it, beauty bears us out of ourselves towards the being in which it shines. It is, in a word—and what a word!—the principle of love. Let a man do for you all that the most ingenious goodness could suggest to a devoted creature, let him pay your debts, save your honour, exalt or create your glory, you will doubtless be led to feel gratitude towards him; but you will not grant to him alone, that tenderness, confidence, and unspeakable trust, which a sudden glance is able to draw from you.

Beauty is the creator of love. And what is it then? What is that charm which respects nothing in our soul, which tames our pride, which makes it a pleasure to us to give our life for nothing, and to halt before God only, at the extreme limit of our liberty. What is it? Can we not know it and learn at least to whom we yield the rule and destiny of our being?

Do not stop before heaven and earth, look not to the sun rising in the shadow of dawn, nor to the sea spreading out its silent waves in immensity,

nor to the mountains, nor to the palaces built by
kings, nor to the ruins made by time. Behold the
face of man, there beauty is, for there is the soul.
Behold it! What will first strike you, is its light. The
face of man is a gentle and living flame which rises
from the eyes and the blood, which brightens, becomes
still, and, even in the deepest repose colours our immobility. Even as the light falling from the stars is
the first beauty of nature, that which falls from the
brow of man is also his highest beauty, and, should
it become extinguished, should the light of the eye
grow dim, the blood become discoloured, we say that
life has departed and given place to death. But the
most admirably lighted face needs also harmony. It
is necessary that light, in order not to lose its splendour upon an unworthy object, should meet with
harmonious lines, proportions which draw all the
features together in unity, and give them, with order,
the second charm which makes the beautiful. Then
and at the same time comes greatness. When we cast
a glance upon the universe, we find there not only
light and harmony, but immensity. A boundless
horizon contains the work of the Creator, and, in spite
of us, leads into the dream of the infinite. Such and
still more vast is the face of man. For the greatness
which is displayed there, although stamped in matter,
is beyond matter; it has neither length, nor breadth,

nor height, nothing measurable or subject to mathematical calculation; it is the greatness of the soul. Something speaks it, and the whole earth, recognising it, is silent before Alexander.

In fine, within the light of man and his greatness, as an action that softens all, appears goodness. Nothing pleases, nothing attracts but what is beneficent, and there is not in nature a leaf of a tree, a dew-drop, a murmur of wind, a shadow, a ray, a silence, whatever it may be, which does not bear with it this character of beneficence. How should man have it not? The masterpiece of divine goodness, the supreme expression of His impenetrable beauty, by his look he brings to our vision the light of God, the harmony of eternity by the harmony of his features, the greatness of the infinite by the sensible greatness of his soul, could it be that goodness alone should fail to shine forth in him? Ah! look at him again, and unless, by the misfortune of chance, you meet only a man unworthy of his own nature, you will easily perceive in his smile and in his tears that last attribute which makes him a child of God. The ancients represented the Gorgon with snakes instead of hair; they were wrong, it would have sufficed, in order to express their thought, to represent the most magnificent human form without any expression of benevolence.

Therefore, Gentlemen, beauty is the expansion of

being in light, harmony, greatness, and goodness; images themselves of the light, harmony, greatness and goodness of God. This is the magic tissue, which, borne by the universe or man, by an angel or a drop of water, draws us out of ourselves by inspiring us with the ineffable madness of love. There lies at once the term of all vision and impulsion, and consequently of the whole life. Our eyes seeking only beauty, and our heart yielding to that alone. Thus Christian theology reduces the final beatitude and perfection of man to seeing God : VIDEBIMUS EUM SICUTI EST,— *We shall see him as he is:* this is beatitude. SIMILES EI ERIMUS QUIA VIDEBIMUS EUM,—*We shall be like to him, because we shall see him :** this is perfection. The sight of the divine beauty will seize us with eternal ecstasy, and that beauty, reflecting upon ourselves, will render our own as perfect as the finite can be when penetrated by the infinite.

But here below, by that alone that we are a life, that is to say a vision and an impulsion, God has sown beauty around us with a profusion that astounds and enraptures our thought. From the star to the grain of sand, from the insect to man, all is light, harmony, greatness, goodness; and infinite littleness itself hides all these characteristics in the imperceptible folds of the creatures which it conceals. The

* 1 John iii. 2.

The Supernatural Life.

eye of an insect is as wonderful as our own, and Solomon halted before the hyssop after having studied the cedar. However, as there is a hierarchy of beings, there is also a hierarchy of beauty; and likewise, as there is a hierarchy of beauty, there is also a hierarchy in the effects produced by it.

Below all the others is material beauty, that which no soul moves inwardly, and which offers to our admiration only the light of colours, the harmony of lines and tones, greatness appreciable by calculation, and goodness altogether limited to the pleasure of our senses. Therefore, however magnificent and true it may be in appearance, our imagination alone seizes it. Our soul cannot love that which has no soul to answer it, and the attraction which urges us towards the scenes of nature, in the depths of woods and on the borders of waters, in the mystery of solitudes and in the noise of tempests, is but an aspiration which is soon exhausted. The flower sees us pass by and speaks nothing to us but its perfume; the tree holds us under its foliage without giving us anything but its shade; and if something more than sensation should be awakened within us before the inanimate marvels of the universe, it is because our mind, more vast than the universe itself, lends to it its poesy and animates it with its sentiments.

"Sooner or later," says Vauvenargues, "we enjoy

souls only," and to find them again, we must return to man. But on account of our structure, at the same time spiritual and corporal, the first search which we make for souls is in the frontispiece of our being, in sensible beauty. There are again the lines, the colours, the shadows, and notwithstanding the perfection of their play, it would be but the universe in a marvellous abridgement, if, under these outer traits, thought did not shine and passion palpitate. In presence of this spectacle of the human face, where the revelation of the invisible world begins, man is troubled; material beauty leaves him master of himself, sensible beauty commands him; he would not have shed a drop of his blood for the universe, he is ready to give it for a creature which has but a day's life, an hour's splendour. A look has decided him, and should language suddenly join that look, should that power, which in the rest of nature is but a sound, a breath, a murmur, a melody, become a living voice which utters the thoughts of a soul, then love, which was but an instinct, becomes transfigured with the beauty which is its cause, and death is silent before a feeling which henceforth can know no other master than virtue. Alas! I am wrong. Time is also its master. Sprung from the senses much more than from the mind, that love depends upon the breath which passes upon the beloved visage. A changing feature, a deepening wrinkle, whatever it may be, suffices to weaken and extinguish it. Often even, the cause altogether remaining, the effect vanishes. We see violent affections fall like a dying wind, and he even who had just now adored, knows not whence comes the indifference which has chilled his transport. It is because sensible beauty has not ground enough of itself, like those shining but shallow lakes, which cannot hold the anchors of the barks that float upon their waters.

Love, like all else that is durable, requires the ocean of eternity. There alone is the principle of that which never changes and never dies. Now there is nothing eternal in man but his ideas whence proceed his virtues; and everything possessing beauty, ideas also possess theirs: a supreme beauty which hides itself behind all the phenomena and all the laws of nature, but which has its principal seat, after God, in the created spirits of which man forms a part. Man sees then within himself, under a form which has nothing material, the primitive elements of all beauty: light, which is truth; harmony, which is order; greatness which is the infinite; goodness, which is the very heart of God. He sees them face to face, he is borne by them beyond time and change, in the region of the immutable, and although always free, he feels there seized by a love which shares the tranquil immortality of the place. It is this beautiful love of intelligible beauty which, shed again upon man, dissolves into the trinity of conjugal, maternal, and filial love, the hallowed source of family, and by family, of the honour and peace of the human race. There, by an amiable and pure mystery, virtue glides into love; virtue, the offspring of ideas, love the offspring of beauty; and both together working at the same time in our heart, a transformation takes place there which is not the last, but which already bears the precursory signs of a more august revelation and a more perfect age. For do not suppose that we have exhausted the hierarchy of the beautiful, or that of the affections which spring therefrom. Even at the height which we have reached, the firmament of ideas, a weakness exists and warns us too loudly of the limits of our life.

Let us consider ideas in themselves, without relation to God, who is their first home, and without relation to man, who possesses the reflection of them; they are no longer but an abstraction which convinces without moving us, which enlightens without touching us. If we bring back their admirable light upon man, it will excite in us feelings which I named just now, passions purified by virtue, love, holy and strong by its ideal principle, but incomplete and fragile by the term upon which its action rests. Virtue comes to

The Supernatural Life. 175

his help, and communicates its immortal breath to him in a certain degree; but the misery of man corrupts or weakens that generous breath, and the most sacred affections of our heart change too often into bitterness and deceptions. The shadows of sensible beauty cross the splendour of intelligible beauty, and this inevitable mixture gives to all our affections, even the most grave, something of powerlessness and decrepitude.

If, weary of our weaknesses, we should turn towards God, the Father of our ideas and virtues, doubtless we no longer meet with the corruptible element; but the divine majesty itself overwhelms and chills us. We see God from too far, and we see him too great. The universe hides him at the same time as it discloses him, and our soul, formed as it is to his image, reveals him only by ideas, that is to say, by general conceptions which unveil his existence and his attributes, without showing his substance or his person. We conclude from the universe interpreted by our mind, that there is a first cause, and, that first cause once acknowledged, we invincibly apply to it, by another necessary conclusion, notions of eternity, infinity, intelligence, justice, wisdom, and goodness. These are sublime prospectives of our soul, a true light, a basis which bears and uplifts our life above all that appears here below. But could we, with that alone, love God with all our heart? Could we give him our blood as we give it for a mother, a wife, a son, a friend, for the soil and the traditions of country? Could we love him as a living being whom we hold in our arms, who speaks to us, who answers us, who says to us: I love you? Ah! doubtless this word is deceitful in the mouth of man; it is often betrayed, more often forgotten; but nevertheless it is spoken: it is spoken sincerely, it is spoken with the thought that it will never be withdrawn. It fills with its immensity a day of our existence, and, when it falls to the ground like a faded flower, we still find for it in remembrance a kind and sacred tomb. Is it so that we love God? Is it so that intelligible beauty, considered in the being in whom it substantially lives, enraptures our faculties and draws from us those vows which subsist even after they are no more? No, if we must believe in our history, we do not so love God, or we love him only inasmuch as we love in loving justice, inasmuch as we love in dying for right, that is to say, that we love him as an idea, with an ideal, but not with a personal affection. When one of the ancients devoted himself for a just cause, God doubtless was not a stranger to his action, since it is God who is the father of justice. But can we say that he was its end? Can we say that he was loved because justice was loved? I believe it, Gentlemen, I do not disavow that initial love of divine beauty; but, assuredly, you do not confound it with that love which sees face to face, which clasps, which promises and gives itself, which makes of the object loved and of the soul loving as it were one sole personality. Let us refuse nothing to ideal love, let us permit it to come as near to God as possible, but let us not grant to it what it never did and what it never was, which is to love God as we love a creature, in adding thereto, above the love of a creature, that of being the first and the last.

Now let us listen to St. Paul: "*Who shall separate us from the love of Christ? Shall tribulation, or distress, or famine, or nakedness, or danger, or persecution, or the sword? In all these things we overcome because of him that hath loved us. For I am sure that neither death, nor life, nor angels, nor principalities, nor powers, nor things present, nor things to come, nor might, nor height, nor depth, nor any other creature, shall be able to separate us from the love of God which is in Christ Jesus our Lord.*"* Hear you these new accents? Do you recognise your heart in these unknown transports? Whence do they come, and what then happened to the world? Ah! what happened to the world? One single

---

* Rom. viii. 35, &c.

thing: the world had seen God. It had seen him, not only behind his works and through ideas, but living with it, in his word, his actions, his physiognomy; no longer hidden in the infinite, but hidden in our own flesh, and throwing into it the light and glory of his personality; no longer under the veil of created beauty, but in the simple splendour of divine beauty. And, as no beauty appears in the world without raising up a new love, Christ, the Man-God, had, as the first effect of his epiphany amongst us, the reward of a love before unknown to man, or, at least, of which he had lost all traces, in losing, with his innocence, the vision of his first days. And when Christ, after having lived, came to die for us, his beauty falling from the cross, took up again, in the depths of charity, the character of infinity which it seemed to have lost; his death illumined his life, and that image, thenceforth invincible, traverses all times under the eyes of those who adore and of those who reject him, master of those who adore him by love which surpasses all other love, master of those who reject him by their powerlessness to love as Christ loved.

Thus, by the vision of divine beauty, and under the impulsion of divine love, is consummated the supernatural life begun in us by the invisible light and movement of grace. Grace acts within to enlighten us. Christ appears without as the object of the light which penetrates within us; grace moves within the hidden springs of our liberty, Christ calls us without as the object of that inner emotion. And no one, however far away he may be, is sheltered from seeing and hearing him. We meet Jesus Christ here below as we meet another man. One day, at a corner of the street, in a solitary path, we halt; we listen, and a voice in our conscience says to us; Behold Jesus Christ. A heavenly moment, when, after so many beauties which it had tasted and which had deceived it, the soul steadfastly sees 'the beauty which never deceives! This may be accused of being a dream by those who have not seen it, but those who have seen it can never more forget it. Whilst in all other contemplation of light, however pure it may be, it falls upon changing and corruptible beings, here the light is eternal, the object unchangeable, and 'the meeting of the one with the other, of the stainless ideal with the perfect real, produces in the soul the highest passion in the highest virtue, a passion that inflames virtue, a virtue that embalms and immortalises passion. Whilst age and the slightest accidents trouble our most cherished affections, the love of God by Jesus Christ lives upon all our woes and all our weaknesses. We may lose it in rising from infancy, because we have conceived it only through another upon the knees of our mother; but, when it has once become our own, the fruit of our experience and our virility, nothing any longer touches in us its ardent certainty. It replaces that which lessens and grows paler day by day. It dwells in our ruins in order to sustain them, in our isolations in order to console them, and when at length we reach the whitened summit of life, in the icy regions that never melt, it is our last warmth and our supreme aspiration. Our eyes may no longer see, but they may still weep, and those tears are shed for the God who shed tears upon us.

It is thus that the love of God has been created upon earth, and it is the love of God that makes all the strength of Christianity, with all its glory. But you will only have an imperfect and even a false knowledge of it, if you do not remark therein a circumstance which gives to it its character and assures its efficacy.

It might be feared that man, having once seen divine goodness, would be thenceforth unable to love any other, and that he would become absorbed in the solitary and sterile contemplation of that incomparable object. For what should we see after God, and what should we love after him? Man had remained great before the universe; could he remain great in the presence of God? And if, in India, the

The Supernatural Life. 181

pretension of seeing him and uniting to him had raised up so many enraptured contemplators of a chimera, should we not expect from the reality, a mysticism still more ardent and more incapable of action? Oh, Gentlemen! you speak truly, and here I understand all the depth of Christian civilisation and of the life which it has made for us. Yes, we might have feared that we should no longer see and love any but God and be divided here below in two irreconcilable factions, that of earth and that of heaven, the one devoted to the ecstasy of the spirit, the other to the voluptuousness of the senses; the one absorbed in the egotism of meditation higher than nature, the other in the implacable effusion of ourselves to the outer world. This is what error would have done; but truth has secrets which error does not possess. Jesus Christ, coming into the world to manifest divine beauty and found divine love, was man and God. He forced us to see ourselves in seeing him, and he could not conquer our love without giving it to mankind. It had been said to us from the beginning, *Thou shalt love the Lord thy God above all things, and thy neighbour as thyself.* But that expression was lost in the darkness of the fall, and the lightnings of Sinai did but grave it upon stone; the heart of man was hardened towards man; it had made of the poor man a slave, and of the weak a stranger. Jesus Christ, the son of God and the son of man, has no longer permitted to us that unnatural blindness; he has given back to us in his person the tie which was wanting to us, and mankind again finds itself in the contemplation even of God. Whoever sees him henceforth sees man with him, and whoever loves him, loves also the brethren whom he chose, not only by his flesh, which is ours, but by his person, which, being all divine, completes in our nature the mystery of its likeness to God. And as it had happened that the least among us had suffered most from the common degradation, it pleased the Man-God especially to raise them up by all the arts of his passage, by being born, living, and dying like them. Jesus Christ has created upon earth the beauty of poverty and misfortune; he has shed upon them, in a double effusion, the glory of Calvary and Thabor; and, withdrawn for a time from the midst of us, he has left them to us as his most living image and his most cherished portion. The poor man sheltered by the very force of Christ, passes respected by generations, and misfortune passes with him, the one and the other calling all ages to take interest in their troubles, by a work which is become the highest function of love and its most magnificent expression.

Thereby, Gentlemen, Christianity has penetrated to the very core the destinies of this world; and the supernatural life, which seemed fitting only to people it with contemplatives, has peopled it with laborious souls, devoted to the condition of all. The divine beauty has illuminated mortal beauty, and the human race transformed can no longer disavow God without disavowing itself. The love of man increases there in the same proportion as the love of God increases, and it lessens by the same cause and in the same proportion. O Thou then, Author of this miracle, sacred tie of the visible and the invisible, inexhaustible source of our present happiness and our future beatitude, of our perfection begun and our perfection to come! O Christ Lord! reign for ever over us; and, if it be permitted to a creature to inspire Thee with courage, reign fearlessly; for, if men may hate love, they cannot dethrone it!

THE INFLUENCE OF
THE SUPERNATURAL LIFE UPON
PERSONAL AND PUBLIC LIFE.

MY LORD, GENTLEMEN,

We have brought human life to the highest point that it can reach here below. After having taken it in the lower regions of instinct, where it is in relation only with nature and produces only passions, we have led it into the spheres of the intelligence, in presence of the ideas of order, justice, and goodness which have God for their eternal seat, and we have seen it expanding there in virtues, that is to say in habits of strength, the offspring at the same time of reason and liberty. At this height already so elevated, a third life appeared. The gleams and emotions of instinct were the elements of the first; the rays and directions of the intelligence were the sources of the second; here we meet with a light still purer and more vivid, a transport more ardent; and, whilst nature was the object of the instinctive life, and ideas the object of the reasonable life, here it is the divine personality which is the term of the soul's vision and impulsion, until upon the open threshold of eternity it contemplates and possesses the very essence of God. Behold the whole man, one and triple in the progressive ascensions of his life, halting at the point which he has chosen, at the lowest even, if he chooses, but finding his happiness and perfection only in drawing towards God, his sole principle and his only end.

Now, Gentlemen, it is not admitted that the supernatural life, which we also call Christian and divine, is here below the highest of all and the most perfect. It is denied; and it must necessarily be denied by those who are not Christians. For life being the expression and measure of all the faculties of man, wheresoever the perfection of life is, there also are the highest faculties, and consequently truth, unless truth belongs to feeble visions and cold inspirations. It is in this manner, that Christianity, accessible to all because it touches all, daily demonstrates its divinity to the world. Invincible on the ground of metaphysics and history, it is much more so on the ground of life, and its adversaries can follow it there only to degrade it by merciless defamations. Such, from the beginning, was the art of the pagans against us. Warned by the power hidden in that new life which appeared before them, they left nothing untried in order to dishonour it. No insult, no calumny did they spare. They invented monsters against the Christians, and Tacitus himself, that grave historian who did more against tyranny by his pen than the sword will ever achieve. Tacitus did not disdain to despise the victims and insult them, because they were Christians. In the last century, unbelief again took up that arm, which time had blunted. Gibbon, painting the *decline of the Roman Empire*, does not fail to impute its shame to Christianity; and Voltaire wrote his *Essai sur les mœurs des nations* to stifle in scorn the historical glory of the Christian nations. The injuries have grown old, but they rise up again from their ashes like all the passions of man, and there is not one amongst us who has not heard their echo. They reproach Christianity with having withdrawn its followers from public life to employ them wholly in the solitary work of their own perfection; they reproach it with having substituted for the agitations of the human forum the selfish peace of conscience and the tranquil charm of intercourse with God. Thence, say they, comes the political inferiority of Christian nations, compared to ancient peoples; an abasement of characters and institutions, a sort of weakness which invites servitude under the name of obedience, and justifies it by the idea of honour.

Happily, Gentlemen, we are no longer in the early days of the Christian era; we have eighteen centuries of history behind us; and the catacombs, which delivered our ancestors to calumny by sheltering them from persecution, have risen from underground with a degree of splendour which enables the world to behold us. To that light I appeal in order to judge Christianity in the life which it has formed, and in the humanity which has issued from that life.

I readily acknowledge that Christianity has exalted the inner man. Whilst the ancients passed their days upon the public places, the Gospel has brought man back to himself, and if it has not created, at least it has enlarged his personal life. Personal life is that converse which we hold with ourselves in our soul. No man can altogether escape from it; whatever he may do to spread himself without, he finds himself within in spite of himself, he speaks to himself, he hears himself; and however mute or devastated may be the intimate solitude of his being, he is nevertheless its host and guardian, but the guardian more or less faithful, the host more or less exact. As we return with pain to a poor and an ill-kept house, so do we return painfully to ourselves when the hearth is empty and the fire extinguished. But when the soul is full, it is for itself its chosen place. The intercourse there is active, because thought abounds; it is sweet, because love is there with thought. Now, when God had become visible to man, and the Gospel had spoken to him, it is manifest that thought should have become elevated, love increased, and that the soul filled to the brim could not escape from the consequence of that plenitude, which was an increase of its intimacy with itself. The man of antiquity had nature only for his horizon, and in beholding the heavens he lighted up the dark lamp of his ideas. The Christian, instead of the heavens, had God himself to contemplate; all became profound in him, even his outer vision. A hidden life grew up in his soul, aspirations unknown appeared there, the world, already of so little account, fell a step lower, and the saints were able to say with truth stripped of all pride; *Every time that I have returned from the midst of men, I have returned less a man.**

Nevertheless personal life is not entirely in the soul; it passes beyond its circle and overflows in the family life. There, near to God and our soul, three persons appear to us: the wife, the child, and the servant; three weaknesses before a single force, which is man. Man abused it before Christianity, because he loved badly and but little; and he knew but imperfectly the joys of family, because he fulfilled its duties but imperfectly. The Gospel, in dilating his heart, gave to him also purer delights and truer affections. The domestic sanctuary became transformed. The wife, who was but a good of

* Following of Jesus Christ.

an inferior order, ill-protected by her too fleeting youth, has become, after God, the highest good of her husband; inflexible oaths have consecrated her destiny; and, virtue crowning her beauty, she has been able to brave age and obtain respect which she bears even to the tomb. Her sons grow up around her as inseparable offshoots; and, as her life declines, theirs, in developing and strengthening, form for her at the same time a throne and a rampart. Maternal majesty succeeds slowly to the royalty of her youth; and that insensible passage from one power to another, always sustained by the inviolable image of Christ, gives to her an immortality which injury may touch but cannot destroy. The mother renews the wife; and one day presenting her children at the altars where she had borne them, she wears her wedding garments again at their nuptial feasts; and already a widow or still a wife, she returns to her hallowed fireside with a second posterity as the vanguard of her death. The child, in his turn, inherits rights and sentiments which Christianity has germinated in the bosom of his mother. Introduced, from his birth, at the gates of eternity, he draws from the holy water poured upon his forehead an invisible but omnipotent character; the hand of his father will touch him sparingly; he will grow up under the roof which has received him, as an ancestor who should one day reign there, and the forethought of his reign will cover him with a shield which makes men strong, at the same time the grace of his age will give him the tenderness which makes them happy. The servant also, covered by the same unction which flows from the wounds of Christ, has not been forgotten in the change of destinies. Formerly a slave, he has become free; a stranger merely, he has become a brother. Instead of stigmas of bondage or marks of indifference, he bears in his visage the honour of useful service, and in his hands the generous grasp of fidelity. His years trouble him not; he knows that gratitude will give him time to die, and that charity will not refuse him the prayer which obtains and the memory which glorifies.

Thus has personal life been enlarged by Christianity. Thus has man, renewed in the ancient blessings, found again in his soul and in his house some traces of the fortunes of his first cradle. Was it a crime not to reject them? Was it an abasement to love with greater love?

I will not however hide it from you, the attack is serious; it is a question of knowing whether personal life has not, among Christians, stifled or at least weakened public life; and, to understand the importance of this doubt, we must render account to ourselves of what that other life is which we call public life.

In personal life, man is in presence of himself; in public life, he is in presence of a people. There, his personal duties and rights, his own perfecting and happiness, command his solicitude; here, the duties and the rights, the perfecting and happiness of a people occupy his thought, and, as a people is evidently more than a man, public life is also evidently superior to personal life. Personal life, alone, touches upon egotism; its very virtues, if they do not take their course in a wider region, easily become corrupted under the empire of a narrow fascination. Would you have proof of this? Open history. Until now it shows us only two kinds of peoples; some formed to public life; the others deprived on every hand of the direction of their affairs and held under the guardianship of a master who permits them only to live without complaining under the laws which he makes for them. Now, for such as these, remark the consequences of their condemnation to personal life.

All public activity being impossible to them, there remains only riches as a means of elevation, and its acquisition as a serious occupation. The spirit of lucre seizes upon hearts. Country, which is the place of great things, changes into a place of commerce. It has merchants for citizens, counters for tribune, and the bank or the exchange for Capitol. Generations there disdain letters, because they do not lead to fortune; and, if nature, always fertile in spite of men, still produces living minds there, we see them, deserters of their gifts and renegades of genius, transform their muse into a courtisan and, in their thirst for gold, betray modesty and truth. Poets aspire to the dignity of financiers, and the sound of glory seems like a dream to them before the chink of gold. Every employ is measured by its salary, every honour by its profit. The greatest names, if there are great names in such a society, appear behind the works of commercial enterprise; and these works, useful in the third or fourth rank, ingeniously take the first, which none disputes with them. Those even who direct the general interests do not disdain to enrich themselves like other men. None know how to be poor, not even the rich. Luxury increases with cupidity, and this irruption of tastes divides the people into two parties which have no longer anything in common; those who enjoy all, and those who enjoy nothing. In the countries of public life, the honour of taking part in affairs excites a generous ambition, and places on the summit of the community a glorious counterpoise to the base tendencies of human nature; whereas here, among those who live for themselves, nothing stops the course of blood and abjection. Cupidity begins, luxury follows, the corruption of morals completes.

For a consequence of riches in nations held in tutelage, not to say servitude, is idleness; and idleness is the inevitable mother of depravity. What is to be done when we can no longer gain our bread or our fortune and, amidst abundance which exempts from all trouble, we see nothing around us which calls upon us to labour from responsibility? Where public life is established, every rich man is a patrician or may become such. As soon as the occupation of his own interests ceases, the general interest appears to him and invites his genius and his heart. He reads in the history of his fathers the example of those who have honoured a great patrimony by great devotedness, and if the elevation of his nature respond even but slightly to the independence which he has acquired or received, the thought of serving the State opens to him a perspective of sacrifice and labour. He must speak, write, command by his talent, and maintain that talent, however noble it may be in itself, by that other power which never suffers an eclipse with impunity, namely, virtue. From his early youth, the son of the patrician, that is to say, of the public man, passionately watches the future which awaits him in presence of his fellow-citizens.

He does not disdain letters, for he knows that it is the supremacy of the mind; with eloquence and taste it is the history of the world; the science of tyrannies and liberties; the light received from time; the shadow of all the great men descending from their glory into the soul which desires to resemble them, and bringing to it, with the majesty of their memory, the courage to do like them. Letters is the palladium of true peoples; and when Athens rose, it had Pallas for divinity. Only those nations who are drawing near their end no longer know its value, because, placing matter above ideas, they no longer see that which enlightens or hear that which moves men. But among living peoples, the cultivation of letters is, after religion, the first public treasure, the aroma of youth and the sword of manhood. It is the young patrician's delight and object; he delights therein like Demosthenes, and devotes himself like Cicero; and all those images of the beautiful, in preparing him for public duties, make already for him an arm against the too precocious errors of his senses. From letters he passes to law. Law is the second initiation to public life. If among the peoples in servitude it leads only to the defence of vulgar interests, among free peoples it is the door of institutions which found or protect. Thus, in elevated meditations and magnanimous habits, the leaders of nations are formed. If riches still produces voluptuous men, it also produces citizens. If it enervates some souls, it strengthens others. But wherever country is an empty temple which expects nothing from us but our silent passage, there rises up all around in formidable idleness a rapid corruption. The strength of souls, should any remain, becomes exhausted in its own dishonour. Empty heads bear the weight of great inheritances, and decayed hearts crawl along after dignities which resemble them. An exchange is made between the corruption of the subjects and the corruption of their masters. These, having nothing more to do, because all is permitted to them, give the impulse to the destruction of morals; and all passes, with unanimous step, to the place where Providence awaits the nations unworthy to live.

Let us, in concluding, add another feature.

In the countries of public life, the citizen is inviolable: that is to say his goods, his honour, his liberty and his person are sheltered from all arbitrary attack, and protected at the same time by sovereign legislation and invincible opinion; law alone controls him; not a dead law, but law living in a magistracy which is itself independent of all except its duties. This profound security, which crime alone can trouble, elevates characters. Each feels himself at home the servant of right by honourable obedience, but mighty against the errors of power, whatsoever they may be. Noble respect for the commonalty, sincere devotedness to an authority incapable of evil, spring from that self-confidence. The whole country breathes freely upon the soil given to it by God; injustices, or such evils as may still be met with, are but the accidents attached to human things, like those clouds which pass over the heavens in the brightest climates. How different is it in the countries where personal life reigns. Even law itself is subject to the caprice of a will which cannot be forestalled; the magistracy, changeable and dependant, obeys there other orders than those of justice: and each, aware that his lot is in the hands of a single man, shrinks into a state of fear which governs his actions, his words, and his thought. The lowest of feelings, namely, fear, becomes the soul of that people. Hypocrisy glides behind fear, in order to lessen it; adulation, in order to disguise it. Between these three vices, which invite and justify one another, hearts become corrupt, characters fall, nothing remains but servitude, and nothing is certain but scorn.

Behold, Gentlemen, in a few words, where the personal life, when it is all alone, leads nations. Man is a complex being, he has received from God a body which gives him natural life; an intelligence which claims from him intellectual life; a soul which raises him to religious life; a family which enables him to enjoy domestic life; but he has also received from the same hand a country, the right and obligation to live in common with his fellow-men; and he cannot abdicate that life more than any other, without falling from himself and giving himself over to unfailing degradation, which is the instrument and forerunner of death. When, then, Christianity is accused of having stifled public life under personal life, a deathblow is evidently aimed at it, since it is to accuse it of being in mankind the propagator of cupidity, of the corruption of morals and the degradation of character.

I declare at once that it cannot be so; I am certain, before I look around me, that a principle of life founded upon the Gospel cannot produce such results, and that the life of Christians, honourable and useful in the order of personal life, has been so also in the order of public life.

Let us turn to history, which must judge us. Since Jesus Christ, history has but two pages, the East and the West. The page of the East is short. Never has it been able to attain to public life. An impure mixture of Asiatic traditions and the Greek decadency, it languished for a thousand years, from Constantine to Mahomet II., between sophists, eunuchs and jesters; and they who had witnessed the birth of truth, after having invented a foolish schism, fell with all the weight of their vileness into the hands of the stranger. The Koran, its conqueror, treads it under foot; and, incapable of regenerating its dust, it continues under another form the lamentable destiny of that part of the world, the first in beauty and for too long the first in misfortune. God has willed to show us, by that solemn example, that even the Christian life, where public life does not exist, cannot sooner or later hinder the desolations of schism and the captivity of its doctrine.

Let us leave the East. A land of servitude and abjection, Christianity has not been able to live there in its true form, which is the Catholic form. Let us leave it there until the day when Providence, satisfied with having taught us such great lessons by its wretchedness, will give back to it at the same time the glory of free peoples and the plenitude of truth. It is the West which is the living centre of Christianity, there we must study its influence on the public life of nations.

Like the East, and before it, the West had fallen a prey to the barbarians; and if, masters of the soil, they had also become masters of the faith, there would have been an end of Christianity in mankind. God did not permit it. Those strong generations which knew only the charm of war and the order of camps, became moved by a civilisation more gentle than their own; and the wave of the Gospel, which already covered the whole Roman empire, rose even to their soul in order to subjugate it. The Sicambre bowed his head before that of Christ; his framée bent before the cross; and those whom neither the Rhine, nor the Alps, nor the Pyrenees, nor the Roman legions had stopped, halted before the voice of bishops announcing to them a God feeble and humiliated by love. At the very moment when the old Greek world, marching to its moral ruin, tortured the Gospel in its persecuting heresies, and in false councils presided over by the imperial power degraded the majesty of the apostolical hierarchy, the barbarians accepted the word of God with simplicity; and, not contented with opening their hearts to him, they raised his bishops to the dignity of statesmen, by giving them a share in public affairs and in the deliberations of the country.

Nevertheless these magnificent rudiments might fall into theocracy. In elevating the episcopacy, and by a necessary consequence the sovereign pontificate, to public life, modern nations had to fear lest they should place themselves temporally under a tutelage which would take from them the direction of things relating to the community. Providence and their traditions delivered them from this peril.

Accustomed, whether as tribes, or as soldiers, to choose their own chiefs, our ancestors preserved even in the submission of their faith the remembrance of their patrimonial liberty, and grafted upon Christianity the institutions which they had brought from their forests. A human monarchy was founded by them side by side with the divine monarchy; a civil and warlike aristocracy side by side with the aristocracy of the episcopate. Tacitus, relating to his age the customs of the Germans, gave this celebrated expression: REGIS EX NOBILITATE, DUCES EX VIRTUTE SUMUNT. "They called their kings from birth, their military chiefs from courage." This expression was as the law of a new world. Whilst the East bent its dishonoured head under Cæsarism and pompously wore the toga of a fictitious nobility, the West became based upon a right of inheritance tempered by election, and created a patriciate by the sword and by the soil; by the sword, which makes devotedness, by the soil, which makes independence. The general affairs, instead of being treated in a council of revocable functionaries or in a senate as null in power as great in name, were to be treated in assemblies which had at the same time the weight and the reality of greatness. The bishops appeared there at the right hand of the barons; and human speech, silent from the time of Cæsar, rose again under a form before unknown to it, at the same time religious and civic, borrowing from the Gospel its unction, from camps their virility, from the nation its sovereign majesty. Thereby, the West suddenly became placed, at the very outset of its career, under the inspiration of public life. The old germanic liberties became allied to the young liberties of the Gospel, the city of modern times was seen rising from the ruins of antiquity; and Rome, already dead, Athens, which was no more, Jerusalem, buried under its curse, all the three extinct but immortal, awoke living in a republic greater and holier than their own, which had Christ for head, the Gospel for charter, the brotherhood of mankind for cement, Europe for frontier, and eternity for future. That which until then had been wanting to Christianity, namely: a people; was given to it. Instead of that bloody corpse which was called the Roman empire, and of that ridiculous society which was called the Greek empire, Christianity had a people, barbarian indeed, but young in body and hale in spirit, able to redeem great faults by great virtues, and sure of its future civilisation in the simple course of time and truth.

All these elements, blended together under new forms, religion and war, birth and election, independence and trust, prepared souls for something which had no name in history, and which has remained famous and cherished after having disappeared. The ancients had known courage, but courage in the service of country in order to defend and aggrandise it, and which, cleaving to no other virtue than itself, to no gentler and wider sentiment, left to the hero only a name, the name of soldier; to glory only a title, contempt of death. A noble work, doubtless, and worthy of respect! The barbarian also was a soldier; like the Greek or the Roman, he despised death, and like them, he loved his country. Nevertheless, baptised in the light and meekness of Christ, he had received from his sword another revelation, a word which it had not spoken to Themistocles, and which the Scipios never heard. The sword said to Themistocles: Be strong for thy country and great for thyself. It said to the Christian: Be strong for thy God, clement towards the weak, the slave of thy word, and even in the fury of blood forget not thy promised love, and think of thy colours. It was chivalry. The knight was the man of war softened by the love of God, and by another tender love sprung from the elevation which woman had received from Christianity. From his infancy, the child of the Christian baron learned to handle arms, but he learned also to love God in order to serve him; and, when a glorious manhood had passed from his heart to his senses, he found in an affection self-respected the all-powerful help of his virtue. Surrounded by his living relations, in presence of his dead ancestors, he came to the altar; there he took oaths wherein God, country, the poor, and love met together without wonder, and with that great day in his memory, he went forth to the unknown fields of the future, uncertain of what he might find in his way, but sure of never betraying his sworn faith and of dying valiantly, if called upon to die. Sometimes he concealed his name, his titles, his glory, but enough remained to recognise the knight; and, even on those occasions when prudence led courage, he said with Tancred:

Conservez ma devise, elle est chère à mon cœur;
Les mots en sont sacrés: c'est l'amour et l'honneur.

Honour, I had well-nigh forgotten it. Honour, throughout the West, was the soul and halo of public life. It was not glory too dear to pride, it was not virtue alone, with its sober inspirations; it was more than glory and more than virtue; a sentiment chaste in itself, an overwhelming fear of all merited shame, the highest delicacy in the most hallowed modesty. It was St Louis a captive and saying to his conqueror, under the threat of death; *Become a Christian and I will make thee a knight*. It was Duguesclin; Bayard; Godfrey de Bouillon; new characters unknown in ancient times, who would have enchanted Plutarch, accustomed as he was to illustrious men, and whose glory, preserved from age to age, still enlightened the degenerate times of Louis XIV. Honour is the equinoctial line of mankind, mankind grows ardent and pure as it draws near to it, it chills and tarnishes as it withdraws therefrom.

Let us now return in thought to the walls of Constantinople; let us enter those lists where ignoble factions dispute before the Emperor for the applause of the multitude. Let us enter those palaces where the theological mania dwells, which persecution stains with blood and effeminacy defames; let us observe those eunuchs who govern, those senators who bend, those soldiers who purchase peace no longer being able to conquer it, that artifice which betrays even those whom it implores to save the Empire; such is the East, that is to say a Christendom where public life had perished.

The West is not, however, fully known to you. Under the sceptre of the Christian kings, below the bishops and the barons there was the people. The people form the foundation of human society. They are formed of those who labour in order to live, because the labour of their ancestors or their own has not yet raised them to the independence of a sufficient patrimony. The people form the living soil of the country. From the people springs all that ascends, to them all that descends returns. Incapable of ruling, because time and science are wanting to them, they have, however, need of public life, either not to be oppressed, or not to wither under the uniform contact of interests and wants. In the West then, by the natural progress of things, the commonalty was founded. The Church had been the first citadel of liberty; the castle the second; the third was the commonalty. A republic obscure, but respected, it had the charter of its rights, it had its council, its chiefs, its militia, and its flags. Under that grave protection, which bound the honour of the weaker classes to that of the stronger, Christian society was formed, not only by the liberal arts, but also by commerce and industry, so scorned by the ancient peoples, a rear-guard of knowledge and probity which took rank in the destinies of Europe, and prepared for itself a more complete accession to public life. What had remained of the slavery left by the old to the new world tended daily to grow less, and at length to disappear. The workman was free, and, warned by the example of the church, the nobility, and the gentry, that every isolated man is a lost man, they formed associations in order to be respected. If they still had masters, they had rights also; and they were no longer alone in presence of riches, nor alone before misfortune.

Thus, from the prince to the peasant, from the

sovereign pontiff to the artisan, a hierarchy grew up in Christian political society where each had his place, his power, and his honour, and where, none being alone, every one was something; a vast assemblage of men divided into nations, which, notwithstanding the remaining vestiges of barbarian customs, realised that form of government composed of monarchy, aristocracy, and democracy, which Aristotle considered to be the best, and of which St. Thomas, after him, gave this description: "The government is perfect in a city or in a people when one alone presides there over all, according to virtue; when he has great men under him who share his authority according to virtue; and, in fine, when the one and the other principate belongs to all, either because all may elect, or because all may be elected."*

But, Gentlemen, it is by acts that the value of men and institutions is decided; let us learn then what were the acts of the Christian West.

Since history has existed, and Moses on the one hand, Homer and Herodotus on the other, traced its first lineaments, we see in the world but one great struggle, that of the most formidable part of the world against the least of all, the struggle between the East and the West. The cradle of man and of his races, a land religious but servile, the East has

* Summa Theol., 1, 2, 9, 105, Art. i.

never ceased to aspire to the domination of all its posterity. The Bible shows it to us founding the first empires, and, from its capitals, menacing the rest of the world. God, who had other designs, opposed Europe to it, and Homer, the historian of his providence, has related to us in the fall of Troy the prelude of the two predestinations. Marathon and Salamis followed one another; the great king turned his back upon those small republics, whose speech reached even to Persepolis and troubled his sleep. Alexander struck the third blow, and from Granicus to the Indus, Asia, amazed, obeyed the word of a Macedonian. It required a thousand years to obtain an avenger. Arabia gave him, and Mahomet, pontiff, legislator and conqueror, appeared, from the pillars of Hercules to Pont Euxine, upon a line of twelve hundred leagues, before Christianity encamped upon the other shore of its destinies. Europe and Christ found again the old enemy, but much more formidable than ever. It was no longer Asia held at its extremities in the bonds of Confucius, and Buddha kept in its centre by the pacific doctrines of Zoroaster; it was Asia armed with a religion in all its youth, and led by a spirit which made of the sword a faith and an apostolate. It was necessary to see falling under the yoke the conquests of Alexander and the Romans, the primitive churches, and even the holy places where rested the bones of the prophets, the memory of the patriarchs, and the still fresh traces of the Saviour of men. A pliant deism, serving as a support to depraved morals, an adoration of God in war and in success, a blind obedience to the lieutenants of Islam ; such was Asia as Mahomet had made it, as it ruled over one half of the world, coveting the other, and from time to time urging thitherward its fanatical squadrons.

Constantinople could but perish there a century sooner or later. It was the West that undertook once more to save the world. Chivalry, following the roads of Alexander, for three centuries arrested there the wave of error. Jerusalem saw again the cross, whilst at the other extremity of the battle-field Christian Spain regained foot by foot the lost ground of civilisation, and shut up in Grenada the remains of a triumph which was to be accomplished under the eyes of Isabella and Ferdinand. I know, Gentlemen, that the eighteenth century has given you another version of these heroic wars; but the eighteenth century was too young for history : it read it as a child reads, and, thanks to the revolutions which have ripened our age, we read as men. Twice in fifty years our armies have found again the remains of the Crusades, and the East has seen its fate decided by Christianity under banners whose colours were changed, but whose ascendancy had no longer any rival. The crescent vanquished under the walls of Poictiers, by the Franks under Charles Martel, on the fields of Grenada by Ferdinand, in the waters of Lepanta by another Spaniard, before Vienna by Sobieski. The crescent has lately received from us the last insult that fortune brings to those whom it has condemned : we have defended it, and the sword of Godfrey de Bouillon has signed the delay granted by Christ to his expiring adversary.

Masters of the East by the road of the Crusades, we have taken it in the rear by a road unknown to antiquity. The Atlantic, open to our ships, has revealed the world to us, and no land, however protected by its ices or its sun, has been able to escape from the curiosity of our science or the ardour of our faith. Jesus Christ has borne his flag over all the seas, bearing therewith the supremacy of those who adore him, and henceforth our laws, morals, arms, commerce, enterprise, all our arts and all our designs hover over the universe, amazed at having for its ruler the narrowest and weakest of the continents fashioned by God. In three centuries, from Augustus to Constantine, Christianity conquered Rome; in five centuries, from Clovis to Charlemagne, it subjected the barbarians, of whom it formed the new peoples ; in six centuries, from Godfrey de Bouillon to Sobieski, it overcame Islamism and reduced it to that weakness which is the forerunner of death; in three centuries, from Vasco de Gama to the still unnamed days of our present life, it has taken possession of all the shores washed by waves, awaiting the inevitable day when it will reign over those portions of mankind which the distance or form of their lands has hitherto withheld from its action. It may, no doubt, be believed that it will perish itself in its triumph, leaving upon its tomb human reason altogether freed from the darkness of ignorance and the mysteries of faith. It is an illusion permitted to our liberty, and whose merit it is useless here to discuss, since it is certain that the Christian West has performed its work, the greatest and most mighty work of which, in six thousand years, history has immortalised the benefit.

Whether, then, we consider the modern nations formed by Christianity from within or from without, in their political organisation or in their expansion, it remains that the public life, far from having been stifled under the weight of the supernatural life, has derived therefrom unparalleled strength, an original sap which has invigorated all things, honour, liberty, letters, the sciences, the arts, and, in fine, has raised the military and civil power of regenerated mankind to a point of greatness which had no example. If the Roman senate could rise again, if Greece could assemble once more on the fields of Elis or of Olympia and devote a day to hearing Bossuet, after Herodotus, ah! doubtless, in spite of their patriotism reviving with them, the generous shades of those great peoples would feel emotions worthy of them and of us, and their applause would greet an accomplished future which they had not even foreseen.

Nevertheless, Gentlemen, does the age in which we live resemble herein the ages which have preceded us? If public life in Europe has shown an admirable development since the time of Clovis, has it not at length become exhausted, and are the Christian nations now anything but ruins devoured by fire, dust driven by the wind? What unity remains to them? and what liberty? Horrible division produces in them at the same time servitude and anarchy. We no longer know whither that great body of Christendom is advancing, which now strikes against unlimited democracy, now against unbalanced autocracy, uncertain of its road and its end, and appearing like a drunken man rather than like a society. If power and right somewhere remain to it, it is not in that portion subject to the authority of the Church, but among the nations which have separated from her by schism and heresy. England in Europe, the United States in America, are the last representatives of order at the same time free and stable. Elsewhere on every hand nations totter, and their repose, if they have any, is but a halt under the hand that represses their respiration. Whence is this state of things? and does it not bear witness to the powerlessness of a religion which no longer knows how to direct or hold its followers?

Gentlemen, in the first place, it is an error, in a question of the influence of Christianity, to break it up, and argue therefrom in favour of the weakness of such or such of its parts, instead of taking it in its total action upon mankind. Doubtless the Catholic Church alone contains Christianity such as God made it, with its hierarchy, its dogmas, its worship, and the full efficacy over souls of its intercession and jurisdiction. But the Catholic Church is not limited, as you suppose, in measuring the outlines of her visible existence. Everywhere, even in the branches ostensibly separated from their primordial stem, the Church holds a regenerating sap and produces effects whose honour belongs to her. She is still the bond of schism, the cement, such as it is, of heresy; whatever substance and cohesion remain to them comes from the blood which she has shed, and which is not yet dry, as we see branches fallen to the ground under the trunk which bore them still holding vegetation sensible to light and dew. Death is not wrought in a day among minds which truth enlightened. For a long time they preserve therefrom gleams which light, impulsions which animate, and to bring them against the source from whence they sprang, and which still acts upon them, it is to attribute to an ungrateful son the merits which he holds from his race, and of which treason has not entirely stripped him. Thus England, which you have named as an exception to the social decadency of Christian nations, what has made England what she is? Is it since her schism that she has founded the institutions to which she owes peace in liberty, honour in obedience, and security even in agitation? It is not so, as you know. The British institutions are the monument of an age when England paid to the apostolic see the tribute which she herself called *Peter's Pence*, and the hand of a catholic archbishop of Canterbury, the faithful and magnanimous hand of Stephen Langton, is for ever marked upon the pages to which remount, from our age to saint Louis, the political traditions of Great Britain. Her spirit and her laws were formed under the influence of the Church, at the same sanctuary and in the same faith which gave her St. Edward the Confessor for a sovereign. The United States in their turn, children of Old England, have carried her customs to the virgin fields of America, and, finding there no trace of antiquity which permitted them to settle under the shelter of an hereditary monarchy and an aristocracy of birth, they have made of that new world a republic animated by a Christian spirit, although imperfect, showing by that example that the public life is not attached to one single form of government, but that it depends especially upon the spirit that animates the peoples and the sincerity that co-ordains their institutions. England reigns at home and elsewhere because she has preserved her public right, slowly and wisely appropriating it to the development of ages, ideas, and wants; the United States reign at home and over themselves, because, as owners of a new land but heirs of an ancient spirit, they have transported the customs of their illustrious mother-country to the shores of their young civilisation. It is Christianity which is the father of these two peoples and the guardian of their charters. Therefore the Comte de Maistre, in speaking of the future of the world, did not desire for England that she should become Christian, but Catholic only; meaning thereby, in his language at the same time orthodox and penetrating, that what is wanting to England, is not the faith that inspires but the authority that guides. In fact, a people traditionally devoted to heresy is not the same thing as a heretic who has so become from his own erring heart. He revolts, the people receive his error; they ignore rather than contradict truth, and, even if all are not innocent by their ignorance, because they are able to overcome it, many have neither the time nor the light which would make them guilty before God. They belong, according to the admirable expression of catholic doctrine, *to the soul of the Church*, children unknown to their mother although borne in her womb, and who still live in her substance as they have sprung from her fecundity.

This remark made, Gentlemen, and it is of the highest importance in appreciating the action of Christianity upon the destinies of mankind, I acknowledge that the greater part of the Catholic people are now in a violent crisis which neither permits liberty to become established nor power to count on the morrow. This is true, it would be as puerile to deny it, as not to see its cause and to accuse Christianity of it. With the exception of England, who has preserved her public right, the people of the European continent have lost theirs, and have not yet recovered or replaced it. They have lost it little by little, under the progressive influence of a sovereignty troubled by the Christian law, and which, employing with persevering skill certain faults and evils in every age, have learned, at length, to despoil the Church, the nobility, and the commonalty of their acquired rights, and reduce them to absolute political powerlessness in order to leave standing and active only the summit of society. If, that work once done, modern nations had accepted it, it would have been the East become master of the world, the Bas Empire arrived at universality, all public life extinct, and the Church herself threatened sooner or later with that terrible legacy which Constantinople has left to St Petersbourg. That could not be. The race of Japhet, Charlemagne, and St Louis, that is to say France, shook down in a single day the work of twenty generations, and we see overthrown, after all the rest, that which had hoped and attempted to be alone great. But, from a misfortune which still lasts, the ruins of public right had brought with it an equal ruin in the faith of nations; Christianity had suffered a fearful lessening of its reign in Europe, and, when the effort of France burst forth to seize its former life again under a new aspect, irreligion directed, or rather led astray, her blows. Whilst the revolution of England was accomplished under the empire of Christianity, our own was inspired by doubt and negation; it destroyed the sanctuary under the pretence of raising France, forgetting that the Romans had placed in the same spot the tribune where their orators spake and the temples where spake their gods. That error has, for sixty years, disordered the world and condemned the most generous plans to failure. Every cause from which religion is absent, and still more every cause that repudiates religion, is a cause to which is wanting the first foundation of mankind. If France had accepted the help of her old faith, a help which advanced before her with disinterestedness whose merit posterity will not forget, doubtless she would nevertheless have suffered greatly, because the establishment of a lost public right is the most laborious work of a people and of an age, but at least she would have preserved in her torments the element of tradition and stability, the effectual presence of God; and Europe, instead of being hardly on the threshold of her future, would already bear the noble weight of an edifice begun in earnest.

But however unfortunate such a situation may be, however fertile in trials it may yet be, its responsibility does not rest upon Christianity, or rather Christianity draws therefrom a new demonstration of its generous influence upon the public life of human societies. On the one hand, the peoples raised up by it have not been able to accept the fate of the East; after a short sleep, they claimed again their public right, being incapable of living out of a regular community and of meekly yielding to repose bought at the cost of all the liberties which they held from their forefathers. They appealed from Louis XIV. to

St Louis, from Charles V. to Charlemagne, as England had appealed from Henry VIII. and Elizabeth to her ancient Parliament. On the other hand, Christianity having been rejected by an ill-conducted revolution, that movement, so just in its causes, has been unable to settle after more than sixty years of efforts; thus witnessing by its failures that it had counted too much upon itself, and that the Christian peoples, whatever they may attempt, will never accomplish anything without the help of the faith which has made them what they are.

Behold now the future, Gentlemen, and behold it under an infallible alternative. Never yet has a nation recovered or replaced its lost public right, save a Christian nation. The Pagan nations were able to raise up illustrious communities in the world; but, the first breath of their public life once lost, they have not been able to restore its inspiration. Neither Athens, nor Sparta, nor Rome, have revived their institutions destroyed and their patriotism extinct; they have, perhaps, still produced great men, they have not produced citizens. Liberty does not rise again from its ashes by its own virtue, and, when England, after the reigns which I have just cited, regained her national right, it was a miracle without example, and which, of itself alone, is a striking proof of the divinity of Christianity. Even as to be born is a natural thing, and to be raised again from the dead is a miraculous thing, so also, to be born to public life is, in a people, the effect of the general laws that govern society; but to regain public life after having lost it, is the effect of a regeneration which comes from above. England has been able to do this because she was Christian, and because, although preserving the heresy which absolute power had imposed upon her, she has rejected with horror scepticism and unbelief. This it was which formed her strength against the political traditions of Henry VIII. and Elizabeth, and it is this which still forms it against the agitations too often powerless in which the Continent struggles before her eyes.

One of these two things then will happen: either Europe will return herself to the light of the Gospel, and by the Gospel which gave to Europe its institutions it will recover its glorious inheritance; or, persevering in the pride of erring reason, it will continue to reject Jesus Christ, and, victim of corruption which will ever increase, it will pass on from chimera to chimera, and from fall to fall, to the repose of those generations which have no longer any other liberty than that of dishonour. Then also Christianity will become the last refuge of great souls. Disgusted with the spectacle of bondage, they will withdraw more and more into the true city of the Christian, which is eternity, and thence they will shed upon the world that glory of saints which shines upon all ruins in order to give to the saddest times a witness and a hope.

Gentlemen, I have ended what I had to say to you in general upon life and its different forms. After having led you from degree to degree even to the supernatural life, the highest of all, I should now speak to you of the virtues which spring therefrom as its fruit and its expression. But already long ago, in another assembly, I have treated of all the supernatural virtues, such as faith, humility, chastity, charity, religion and holiness, not neglecting also to show the influence of these virtues upon human society as to right, property, authority, family and political economy. The work is then accomplished, and there would remain to me here only to speak to you of the means established by God to communicate to us the supernatural life. I mean the Sacraments, which I have touched upon but once in regard to the intercourse between man and God, and under their most general aspect. Shall I be permitted to expose this doctrine to you, and thus to complete, after more than twenty years, the whole apology of the Christian faith ? I know not, but whether I may meet you here again or never more see you, whether God close my mouth or open it once more, I shall not leave you without feeling happy in having wrought a part of my ministry in this city, which was the cradle of my order, where St. Dominick had the first vision and the first friends of his thought, and where I have met, in a worthy archbishop, the successor of that illustrious Foulques, the benefactor of my fathers and the shield of the Faith.

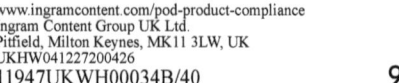